You remember your first mountain in much the same way you remember having your first sexual experience, except that climbing doesn't make as much mess and you don't cry for a week if Ben Nevis forgets to phone next morning.

'Who else would speculate on how Scottish hill-walkers would cope with bears and wolves, propose a helpline for the people who can't go into an outdoor shop without buying an aluminium water-carrier or loop-stitched socks, or describe a Hogmanay weekend in Torridon as a "raging success with only one person burned and two slightly bruised"? . . . the book resembles a jampacked rucksack in rainbow colours . . . Roll on the next 50'

GLASGOW HERALD

'Keen eye and sardonic humour . . . I laughed a lot: she clearly knows her hills and hill-walkers, there is a lot of sound sense among the sallies'

SCOTLAND ON SUNDAY

'A hilarious account of Munro conquests . . . brings the hills alive with elegies that are unmistakably her own . . . an antidote to those who see mountains only as places of solemn homage and grave endeavour and a revelation for those who wish for walking books which rank enjoyment at least as high as achievement'

NORTHERN ECHO

Muriel Gray was born and bred in Glasgow. A graduate of Glasgow Art School, she spent three years working as an illustrator, and a further two and a half as a designer at the National Museum of Antiquities. She has contributed to various magazines, television shows and radio programmes and was the presenter of *The Tube* in all of its five series and of *The Media Show*. She has also contributed columns to *Time Out*, the *Sunday Mirror*, the *Sunday Mail* and the *Sunday Correspondent*, and she now runs a television production company in Edinburgh, where she has also been Rector of the University. Muriel's great love is being in the Scottish Highlands. She is currently trying to grow a beard.

THE FIRST FIFTY

Munro-Bagging Without a Beard

Muriel Gray

CORGI BOOKS

THE FIRST FIFTY
A CORGI BOOK 0 552 13937 8

Originally published in Great Britain by
Mainstream Publishing Ltd.

PRINTING HISTORY
Mainstream edition published 1991
Corgi edition published 1993

Copyright © Muriel Gray 1991

Photographs © Ross Murray
pages 234–5, Colour section page 7
Photographs © Rod Stein
pages 20, 57, 100, 194–5, 240–1,
Colour section pages 6, 8
Additional photography Muriel Gray

The right of Muriel Gray to be identified as author of this
work has been asserted in accordance with sections 77 and 78 of
the Copyright Designs and Patents Act 1988.

Conditions of Sale

1. This book is sold subject to the condition that it shall not, by
way of trade *or otherwise*, be lent, re-sold, hired out or otherwise
circulated in any form of binding or cover other than that in
which it is published *and without a similar condition including this
condition being imposed on the subsequent purchaser.*

2. This book is sold subject to the Standard Conditions of Sale
of Net Books and may not be re-sold in the UK below the
net price fixed by the publishers for the book.

This book is set in 12pt Linotype Garamond 3 by
Phoenix Typesetting, Ilkley, West Yorkshire.

Corgi Books are published by Transworld Publishers Ltd.,
61–63 Uxbridge Road, Ealing, London W5 5SA,
in Australia by Transworld Publishers (Australia) Pty. Ltd.,
15–25 Helles Avenue, Moorebank, NSW 2170,
and in New Zealand by Transworld Publishers (N.Z.) Ltd.,
3 William Pickering Drive, Albany, Auckland.

Reproduced, printed and bound in Great Britain by
Biddles Ltd, Guildford and King's Lynn

To those I love, who shared
their soup with me at the cairn

Contents

Introduction

IF YOU WALK UP MOUNTAINS FOR FUN, THEN A good idea is to keep the dark secret to yourself when it comes to birthdays or Christmas. The reason is that relations and friends put you into the 'easy' category of present buying, which is probably why you're miserably flicking through this book.

They will automatically take their cheque book into an outdoor shop. This is not a shop that trades beneath a flapping canvas on the edge of the pavement, but a shop where even the carpet is made of Gortex, and the assistants shift restlessly from one trainer-clad foot to another as they dream of being somewhere other than here beneath the striplit rows of anoraks and attractive wall displays of bum-bags.

These shops also display books on climbing and walking, and perhaps you're reading this bit as you stand in such a shop somewhere between the ice-axes and the fuchsia skiing tube socks. The problem is that your friends and relations will quickly lose patience in trying to decide if you already have a Swiss army knife, or whether a hat with a pompom may get you beaten up in the Kingshouse Hotel, and just go for the easy option of buying you a book with a man with a beard on the cover. You can't go wrong with books that have men with beards on them. I know. Relations have bought me hundreds. The man will be on top of a particularly dramatic-looking mountain, and no matter how pompously the hairy author writes about his tedious exploits and mind-numbingly dull companions, the book will always be bought for the pictures. So just as you may have flicked through old *National Geographic* magazines as a teenager looking for the pictures of naked tribes with huge breasts and penises, you can flick through the bearded man's book looking for interesting peaks and scary photographs of people hanging off rocks.

I shan't be at all offended if you now flick through to see what hills I've decided to discuss and decide you most certainly never want to read or own such a book. After all, it's not important if you like or dislike it. Your Aunty Helen or your flat-mate Alan will almost certainly buy it for you next time you have a birthday and you will have to thank them and put it in the warehouse with the rest of the outdoor books.

Tough titty. You should have taken up golf.

Why Me?

Y OU REMEMBER YOUR FIRST MOUNTAIN IN MUCH
the same way you remember having your first sexual
experience except that walking doesn't make as much
mess and you don't cry for a week if Ben Nevis forgets to phone the next morning.

But, like losing your virginity, it's hard to recreate that
nascent flavour of exhilaration when you realize that by
determination, corporeal suffering that involves wheezing
until your lungs feel like a laboratory beagle's, you've done
something you didn't believe physically possible. Unfortunately, unlike losing your virginity, Munro-bagging
stays just as sore every time you do it.

To the sofa-bound layperson it may just be a wind-
blown cairn, grey and dismal except for its decorative
orange peel, but to you it's nirvana. It remains constantly
awe-inspiring that your feet, and a flask of tomato soup,
can take you to the remotest and most primevally beautiful parts of our country, from where those who sit in
aluminium chairs a foot from an open hatchback listening

to Gary Davis's *Bit In the Middle* are excluded by their sedentary nature. It's a sensation that once felt has to be repeated for the rest of your life, or until the end of Gary Davis's *Bit In the Middle,* whichever comes first.

Ben Arthur, or The Cobbler, was my first. Not a Munro, but 15 years ago, at the tender age of 16 when I should have been in Sauchiehall Street choosing stripey socks, I could be forgiven for never having heard of Sir Hugh or his damned tables. Never mind Munros – had I known how hard The Cobbler was to be I would have stayed home and watched a black-and-white movie on telly with my mum. To this day I am the kind of hill-walker who starts the day with a face like a football with slits cut in it for eyes. The early start so essential to claiming that peak has never become easier. But to impress the man I loved at the time, I emerged from his friend's beat-up Mini at the car park opposite Arrochar thinking, 'I am not going to lose this very handsome boyfriend who wants to do this instead of going to Kelvingrove Art Gallery for a look at the Rembrandt and a snog. I will die as soon as we start to walk.

'He's bound to leave me to rot,' I surmised, 'and get off with that tart from the textiles department at Glasgow School of Art that seemed to fancy him. I'll bet she goes hill-walking,' I thought as I caught sight of my figure in a donkey jacket and waterproof trousers in the car's wing mirror. Mind you, with thighs like a Tyrannosaurus Rex I suppose the brazen hussy would have been well suited to the hills, and I bet even her hair would mat like felt under a balaclava for eight hours.

So I admit it was sex that drove me on that winter's day, through rain at first, turning to sleet as we passed the tree line and into wet driving snow as we neared the top.

Winter hill-climbing has tortures all of its own. Never go first in thick snow unless you have legs that are six feet long and thighs of iron. Breaking the path is murder. For some reason I imagined this was my task, kicking pathetic little holes up the gradient with all the effectiveness of a toddler having a tantrum in a supermarket.

In those days of misplaced student feminism I was terrified of being seen as a feeble girlie. God knows why. These days I'd sing *On the Good Ship Lollipop* and speak like Bonnie Langford if I could get one of the lazy bastards with beards to carry my rucksack. Unfortunately, 20th-century men are shrewd, reserving their manly acts of chivalry only for those who resemble Brooke Shields. Since my hair does indeed mat like felt under a balaclava, I usually end up carrying their rucksacks.

But, way back then, I genuinely believed that physical weakness was a sign of inferiority, and so I would struggle away, silently hyperventilating to keep up with these men who weighed 13 stone next to my eight stone, and whose legs were so big they could get to the top in three strides.

Wrestling with the thought 'I want to go back' is fundamental to hill-walking, and of course all the bearded experts with accents like Sussex vicars will advise you that you must always know when to turn back. If you are 16 and trying to get your boyfriend to think you're great, the answer is that you may only turn back when all the other members of the party before you have lost two or more of their limbs and decide it's time to call it a day.

I imagined it with horror.

'I see you've lost a leg there, Ian.'

'Aye, Alec, but it's OK. It's only knocked the schedule out by ten minutes. We'll be at the top in an hour. How's that grievous spinal injury you've just incurred?'

'No problem, Ian. I'll just crawl up to this coll with my one good arm and take a bearing. Is that Ladhar Bheinn over there or are the severe facial lacerations I have been unlucky enough to receive clouding my vision? Any Lucozade left?'

This too has changed in my maturity. Now I make sure we travel in my car. There is no greater incentive for calling the shots than cheerily telling the chaps who want to continue up a mountain in a force-ten gale and blizzard that they may make their own way back from Torridon to Glasgow.

However, I digress. Struggling up The Cobbler as I was on that day, I was not only wrestling with the thought 'I want to go back', I had started to form the thought 'Perhaps I'll die'. The worst aspect of this thought at 16 is that Mountain Rescue may remove your balaclava before you've got to a hair brush. 'Nasty,' the mountain leader would say. 'Hair matted like felt.'

But no-one had explained the pain barrier to me at that age. It is the most astonishing feeling, that only someone as chronically unfit as I am can experience, to come through the painful fog into the bright sunlight of new energy. The medical explanation is to do with metabolism and stamina. My explanation is that I remembered there were to be pork pies soon. The arrival at the top of that small hill meant everything to me. Not only lunch and a chance to sit down on a rock, but the fact that in spite of my grossly sedentary nature, I was actually there on the snowy summit with the boys.

What could have been more thrilling and rewarding than to have conquered pain, exhaustion and the humiliation of looking like a navigational engineer, to stand on this beautiful, silent top drinking in the view across Loch Long to Ben Lomond? I was elated, and have continued to be every time I haul myself to the summit of anything higher than the top deck of a bus.

It seems ludicrous now that I found such a short walk so arduous. But it's important to realize that most teenage girls take exercise only when dancing round their handbags at discos looking for men over six foot.

The mountain that started it all: The Cobbler

Stamina is often psychological and if you wander the Munros in all seasons, you'll find yourself calling on it in a bewildering variety of situations.

I'm grateful that it was a boyfriend who gave me that first taste of the hills, and not my parents. I often come across small family units wandering through the heather, a tweedy university lecturer of a father setting the pace, followed at a respectful distance by a bespectacled, lank-haired mother wearing an acrylic hat and towing two sulky miserable children. Judging by their disgruntled demeanour, these poor mites will doubtless stop walking the hills the moment they grow their first pubic hair, and I grieve for all the pleasure they will miss as adults if they put the hills aside as one would childhood caravan holidays in Girvan. Only take your children up mountains if they beg and scream to go. A pleasure you discover for yourself is worth far more than one you were expected to enjoy by your elders. And how can you enjoy a cold pint in the bar afterwards if you're only seven and a half?

Apart from anything else, hill-walking is not quite as wholesome as your bearded, Fair Isle tank-top brigade would have us believe, so exposing your children to some of the tartan-shirted bears one finds relieving themselves behind cairns is perhaps to be avoided.

So The Cobbler got me going and I haven't stopped since.

I am always mortally offended when people express surprise that I am a keen mountaineer. I have no idea why a job in television should give strangers the impression that my idea of fun is to hang around night clubs sniffing nose candy. But they most definitely register disappointment when I tell them that I'd swop without hesitation a ticket to some God-awful film première and party that minor celebrities are expected to attend for a night by the log fire at the Cluanie Inn discussing whether the South Kintail Ridge really deserves to have seven Munros.

I have great pity and sympathy for my misguided colleagues who imagine they are living the high life in London, mooching from champagne reception to book launch party in the grim pursuit of having their photograph in a Sunday supplement magazine alongside a member of the England football squad. That is as near to my idea of Hell as possible, perhaps with the exception of being stuck in a lift with Simon Bates.

I can think of no greater privilege than to be able to live and work in Scotland, where at every possible opportunity one is able to jump into a car and head for one of the most beautiful and accessible areas of wilderness in the world. In the same time it takes someone to get from Central London to Heathrow airport in a Hackney cab with a fascist behind the wheel, I can be cruising over Drumochter Summit well on my way to Heaven. I can only thank my parents from the bottom of my soul for not bringing me up in Belgium.

So this is not a guide book, but a grateful celebration of something I love. Indeed sometimes when I find myself all alone amidst scenery so grand and profoundly inspiring that it sweetly forces me to examine my life and values, love is almost an inadequate word. Experience is really only a series of near misses and major triumphs from which you learn, and the only way to become a competent mountaineer is to scramble up mountains in every possible weather, and in every season.

Hopefully those of you who want to start wandering into the wilderness, but who for one reason or another are unable or unwilling to grow a beard, will be encouraged by the fact that someone as unlikely as the spindly-legged little sprat that I am has done so. I offer you my observations only as an amateur, and will be delighted if they encourage you to explore and fall in love with the mountains of Scotland. That is, unless you're a complete dick-head that leaves litter at the top, parks on farmers' private roads and doesn't care what mountain you're on as long as you can tick it off in

the book. Please put this book down immediately, it isn't meant for you. You'll be after the train-spotting volumes which you'll find over there next to the pet care books.

The rest of you may read on.

You Mean You Do It For Fun?

ALTHOUGH YOU'RE PROBABLY SICK OF HAVING dull old buffers in moleskin breeches telling you how the hills are full of very different people than they remember, it happens to be true. When the Scottish Mountaineering Club brought out a comprehensive guide cunningly titled *The Munros* in 1985, little did they suspect that the XR2 drivers would steer their crates away from the ski-slopes and head for the un-pisted hills – hills previously only visited by those of us who smugly regarded them as a spiritual escape, a haven of solitude, rather than a sport requiring the purchase of expensive consumer durables and matching accessories.

I had no idea what a Munro was when I started mountaineering. Hence years later a mad-eyed fellow walker in a bar at Crianlarich surprised me by expressing dismay on my behalf that I had 'wasted all that time' climbing up lesser peaks like the mountains of Assynt, and been foolish in the extreme to have scaled some peaks several times as I had, and indeed still do. The real challenge, I

was told by this loony, was to complete the Munros. I
thought he meant a chain of butcher shops and my mind
raced as to why I would be required to visit meat shops
around the country examining best cuts of Scottish lamb.
I was put in the picture. The chap wasn't quite sure who
Munro was, but he was sure about one thing. Other peaks
don't count, he informed me conspiratorially, wiping the
foam of his Guinness from his beard.

And so, as if by prophecy, the SMC's book appeared
in every walker's Christmas stocking, mocking my expeditions up smaller but beloved mountains. Here at
last was a book listing all the Munros, giving the reader
the perfect tool of one-upmanship. 'How many have you
done?' echoed in the beer bars of major cities.

Just as lots of men waste thousands of hours and
pounds pointlessly on hi-fi equipment, since all they
do is get home and play Dire Straits, so did lots of men
spend thousands of pounds and hours on Gortex creations,
boots, tents, axes and foil bags, only to trudge about on
boring lumps in the mist to get another unpronounceable
name ticked off in the SMC's book.

No, of course they wouldn't dream of going up Suilven.
It's not a Munro, is it? Much better to tick off something
a couple of hundred feet higher even if it's as exciting
as walking about on the roof of the Scottish Exhibition
Centre.

Suddenly there was no talk of the beauty of the hill,
wildlife encounters, or comparisons with other peaks in
the bars at the foot of favourite mountains. Instead the
properties of Yeti-gaiters were discussed religiously, cars
were sized up and anecdotes about each other's very

interesting jobs in computers were swopped. And above all, there was the burning question. 'How many have you done?'

But who can blame Mrs Thatcher's young consumers for wanting a bit of wilderness too? After all, I've been tutted at often enough on the hill by the beards, presumably for being a bottle blonde with a bit of lip salve on. And sometimes it can be a relief to meet these consumer magazine fanatics at the top if all you've met so far is a miserable family who look like depressed social workers. It's almost comforting listening to Maitland and Crawford talking about £1,500 solar rucksacks, after half an hour at a cairn listening to Mr Social Worker make the two junior social workers name alpine flowers they've spotted on the way up in alphabetical order.

'It was a Cryptogramma crispa, Daddy!'

'That's correct, Rebecca, now write it down in your notebook and eat your lentils.'

Economics have certainly changed the face of the modern mountaineer. No longer exclusively an escape from the dole queue in Glasgow, it's now an escape from the office, and a sport to discuss over the dinner tables of Hyndland along with windsurfing and skiing.

But if the original pioneering mountain men have seen radical changes since they strode in a manly fashion up the crags in the 30s, the changes since the 70s have been just as fascinating, in more than just economic terms.

The mountains really were the domain of men. Men who roamed in noisy packs wearing tartan shirts, who prided themselves on their hardiness, and who sniggered

about the women left at home in the same way Les
Dawson discusses his mother-in-law.

But over the last two decades couples started sneaking
on to the hill. Women decided that the men coming home
flushed and smelling of 80-shilling beer had been spending a more exciting day than the one they'd been wasting
window-shopping for pine dressers. Articles about the
great outdoors started to appear in women's magazines
between the shortbread recipes and the advice on orgasms.
Hence the hairy tartan pack members started to find
that their wives and girlfriends wanted to come too,
and the matching his and hers kagoul came into its
own.

Of course the older Arran-knit-jumper couples, who
contribute to the letters page in the *Scots Magazine* with
photographs of peculiarly shaped rocks they've observed,
had always been there. I have great affection for them.
They've been sharing binoculars for years in the pursuit
of the snow-bunting and a good spot to brew up.

The couples new to the ridges were quite different.
Students, young marrieds, young professional couples
who should have been watching the rugby or out buying compact discs. They had cars and could afford to
stay in hotels, preferring to put on some casual cottons
from Next in the evening and take their meals in the
dining-room, instead of standing in the bar eating cheese
toasties beside gently reeking climbers.

I started to notice them when I became aware of
people staring at my donkey jacket in the car park. I
also noticed that the women never wore balaclavas. The
great pity is that this is practically the only time one

sees women on the hills. The male tartan packs are still there, presumably having persuaded their women that a pine dresser is an important purchase, but there is no equivalent pack of women roaming the heather smelling of talcum powder instead of sweat and curry.

I'm as guilty. I only ever go to the hills with a man, a group of mixed sex friends or completely alone. I can't recall ever walking with a large group of women.

I don't think there is a sinister reason for this, merely a traditional social one. Walking expeditions are usually arranged in the pub, when someone, invariably a man, will express a desire to conquer a particular ridge or peak. This is followed by a debate on how to get there and a telephone poll of those one knows to be interested and free to go. Women, for whatever reason, are only ever included in this rounding up if they are one half of a climbing or walking couple. Often, like my first hill-walk, the women would be there under sufferance and struggling away on their own trying hard not to let the side down. I know this is changing, not just because my female friends have all now bought their pine dressers, but because fleecy tops now come in pink.

I know women now who leave the men standing with their speed up a hill, and who can be relied on to take map bearings far more accurately in the mist than their hairier companions. But I'm anxious that more women realize that just because the whole mountaineering scene reeks with testosterone, an atmosphere that is irritatingly promoted continually by all the most celebrated climbers and walkers, they should not exclude themselves from the joys of the hills. It's hopeless saying to women who

don't get invited on walks by male friends, join a club. I would rather have my nipples cut off than have to sit in a mini-bus with a bunch of people who ask the driver to turn off the radio and think committees are a good idea, in the vain attempt to find kindred spirits. Fine if you want to stop for a nice cup of tea on the way home and discuss toilet facilities in Gairloch, but perhaps not the place to find wild, exciting and funny companions who can be reckless and responsible at the same time. I will of course stand corrected if someone can prove they met Harrison Ford on a mass ramble up Lochnagar, but my experience of organized walking clubs has been less than satisfactory for someone who wants to push themselves to the edge of their ability, and have a hoot in the pub later.

The best advice I can offer is to start walking with someone more experienced, man or woman, and then after about 20 mountains break loose and go on your own. Nothing will give you more confidence as a mountaineer than to have successfully taken decisions on your own, and to have experienced the true nature of solitude by having no-one to half a Mars Bar with. For inexperienced and insecure women, this is the best way to gain confidence to initiate hill-walks instead of just waiting to see where the lads are off to this weekend and tagging along. Hopefully, if enough women wake up to the fact the hills are for them, then we'll see another swing away from the traditional macho mountaineer image that Munro-bagging has yet to escape from.

I certainly don't want men to start spending their Saturdays shopping for pine furniture instead of us. I just ache for a better balance of social and sexual mix on the hills; young women as well as young men, and people without money alongside those who can't get out of their Volvo unless their Gortex jacket matches their gaiters.

Having said that, don't all choose the same Munro at once, especially if it's one of my favourites. I'm getting cheesed off pursuing solitude, only to find the summit of a mountain less like a wind-blown sanctuary of peace, and more like the check-in desk for Palma at Glasgow airport on Fair Friday.

But then, in eulogizing about my love of the mountains and my desire for the democratization of their walkers, I forgot to mention one tiny thing. I'm a grumpy, selfish old cow and I want the hills to myself.

Ben More Assynt to Conival

Ben More Assynt; 998m; (OS Sheet 15; 318201); M140.
Conival; 987m; (OS Sheet 15; 303199); M154.

I LOVE WALKING ALONE, BUT SOMETIMES MISS having someone to share it all with. For a start, how can you enjoy the standard argument at the summit about the identity of the peaks you can see? Few mountain tiffs are more heated than two or more hill-walkers fighting to make the others realize why that can't possibly be Ben Nevis over there, or to be the first one to correctly name the pointy little sod all on its own on the far horizon. In such a squabble the answer is always Schiehallion. Remember that. It saves time.

I decided to spend a few days off work one September, walking on my own. I fancied Assynt, but then I have always fancied Assynt. If Assynt was a boy I'd have knocked it to the ground with a rugby tackle and pulled its trousers down years ago.

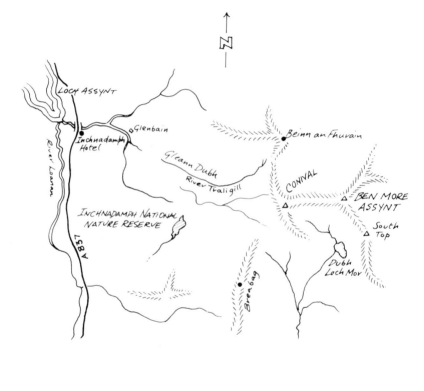

The most magnificent aspect of this wild area is its
savage moorland, flat but pitted with sparkling water-
lily-clogged lochans, interrupted by curious peaks that
assume a grandeur far in excess of their true height. Plus
it bears a sublime coastline, white sand and a tumbling
turquoise ocean that would make poets weep. Certainly
Norman MacCaig wrote about it extensively, Assynt
being an area that has touched him through decades.
I'm not sure if he weeps about the coastline, but I'll bet
he's had a paddle.

The fascination of the area is endless, from the delights
of a magnificent coast road from Lochinver to Kylesku via
Drumbeg, to the impressive Eas a' Chual Aluinn waterfall
at the head of Loch Glencoul, and of course the breath-
takingly extravagant mountain architecture.

One rather melancholy aspect is that its perfection has
attracted the variety of tourists who do not wish to go
home and who have gradually but steadily replaced the
locals over the last 20 years. It's impossible for someone
locally born and bred, invariably with a low-paid job,
to compete on the property market with those who
can realize over £100,000 for a shabby little terraced
house in London. Hence few owners of houses, shops,
hotels or petrol stations boast anything remotely like a
Scottish accent. But if you can live with the reality that
Sutherland is now a region in Surrey, then the incongruity
of the new inhabitants will not mar your pleasure in
beholding the majestic terrain amidst which they arrange
their lawns round stone herons and name their ex-croft
houses 'Windsor'. Who can blame them? Had I lived all
my life in a rurally uninspiring, overpopulated country

like England, I daresay I would be whimpering to live in Sutherland. I just can't help wondering as more and more elderly non-Scots buy holiday and retirement homes there, where the elderly locals are retiring to.

Since I'd scrambled up all the sexiest visible peaks like Quinag, Stac Pollaidh, Canisp and Suilven, and since Munro fever was newly burning in my veins, I headed for the two sneaky Munros hiding behind the Inchnadamph National Nature Reserve: Ben More Assynt and Conival.

The obvious starting point for the walk is from the Inchnadamph Hotel, and if you have enough cash to stay there it couldn't be more convenient. It's not wildly expensive but it's by no means a climbers' pit either. I arrived to find lots of elderly couples in suits and twin-sets taking sherry alongside dour fishermen. I had hoped for a bar full of burly, handsome geology students, since Assynt is a geological Mecca for those handy with a little hammer. But university term hadn't started so I was stranded in an atmosphere not dissimilar to an *Antiques Road Show* in Swindon.

I'm not sure if I dribble maniacally while I eat, but I have begun to notice that whenever I travel alone people completely ignore me. Hence when I finished my breakfast the following day and pulled on my boots, I had spoken only twice in 24 hours: once to apologize to a policeman for dreamily doing 68 mph on a single carriageway on the A9, for which I was forgiven, and secondly to check in and ask when dinner was.

Everybody else spoke to everybody else at dinner. In fact they were practically exchanging addresses across tables by the time the coffee was served. Even the waitress ignored me, choosing to ask the old couple at a table some distance away if they had enjoyed their lunch in Lochinver, while absently taking my order. It's worth remembering something before you set out for the Highlands with a romantic notion of bustling, lively inns, crackling log fires, impromptu music and song, and wise local characters to inform and amuse you about their landscape. Almost all Scottish hotels are like municipal old folk's homes, with miserable-looking senior citizens propped up in chilly residents' lounges waiting for an afternoon tea or a run to the nearest town in their beige Maestro. Soup of the day is always tomato and the fireplaces will be bricked up and sporting a one-bar coal-effect electric monstrosity that you will need permission to switch on. Of course I do not accuse the Inchnadamph Hotel of following such form, and I'm sure when it's full of students pouring beer over their heads and trying to abseil down to breakfast from the second floor, it can be a warm, lively little place. However, on the occasion of my visit I would have had more fun staying in a survival bag in the car park.

I took the packed lunch and silently set off up the farm track at the back of the hotel, leaving the other residents to plan which lay-by they would choose, where they could open the car doors a little and read a newspaper until it would be time to return for afternoon tea and scones.

You can see a grand Victorian house on your left on the other side of the river as you walk, but it's not the most important one in the area. The Vestey family, who own all the juiciest parts of Assynt, have a lodge at the back of Lochinver on the way to Suilven.

Called Glencanisp Lodge, it's set in beautiful grounds with a loch that reflects the mountain perfectly into their sitting-room on the odd occasion when there's anyone there to enjoy it. So if you want to scowl at the herbacious borders of fabulously rich absentee landlords, it's an ideal spot to mooch past and sulk.

The walk into Conival is very straightforward, but I was irritated that I failed to find the caves marked on the ordnance survey map on the southern side of Gleann Dubh, and I dared not retrace my steps for fear of leaving insufficient time to complete both peaks. This is a hot area for potholing, a pastime only marginally more baffling than why people think Jim Davidson is funny. I put this to some potholers once.

'Well why do you go up hills?' they riposted smugly.

'Because it mixes the challenge of strenuous exercise with the reward of an amazing view, a fuller understanding of the geography of our land and intoxicating amounts of fresh air.'

'Oh,' they said, and became disappointingly silent, leaving me to this day waiting for a plausible excuse for their cramming themselves into hideous, airless, dangerously confined spaces with no certainty that there's a way out. Mind you, people do that on a daily basis when they travel British Rail. At least the potholers get to wear a helmet with a light on it and don't have to listen to a bored Yorkshireman read out the entire buffet menu each time a luckless passenger joins the train.

So I missed the caves but plodded on up the narrowing track, making the peculiar mistake of crossing the river

and climbing straight up a huge boulder field. I noticed
two people were behind me at some distance, but just
in case they had binoculars I stopped and tapped one of
the rocks professionally, as if I meant to be there. Don't
take my route whatever you do. The SMC book quite
correctly tells you to follow the glen up on to the ridge,
and if you shun that advice and copy my route you too
would be floundering around on a near-vertical field of
unstable and slippery rocks designed specially by God to
break legs.

The slight detour only made the top sweeter, and
after the confines of the glen, Conival surprises by its
marvellously open aspect. From here you can see across
to the Glencanisp forest and, more rewardingly, into the
wild interior lands to the east. These really are hidden
peaks since they cannot be viewed from the road and,
indeed, Ben More will not come into view until you
have claimed Conival. But if not as dramatic as some
of their lower fellow mountains in the area, they are
comely grey, scree-topped peaks, and stunning in the
vantage point they offer to view vast tracts of Sutherland's
wilderness unseen by the tourist.

The logical route to Ben More Assynt means carrying
on round the ridge and then retracing your steps back to
Conival for the descent. For variety and a much bigger
walk, a fit Munroist could descend on the east side of Ben
More, skirting the edge of Beinn an Fhurain to pick up
a stalkers' path at Loch nan Cuaran.

However, I was rather looking forward to meeting the
couple I could see gaining on me as I left Conival for
Ben More. I worked out that if I had my lunch on the

summit of Ben More, I would be halfway back along the ridge when we would meet. No cardigan-clad, lay-by dwellers these. As far as I'm concerned anyone I meet out on the hills is a comrade and conversation would be more than welcome. Where had they been? Where were they going? Where were they staying? Had they found the caves?

I finished my hotel packed lunch, and set off back along the ridge to greet them. We met as predicted, halfway along. It was a couple in their thirties.

'Hello there,' I cried cheerfully from 15 feet away.

They didn't even look up as they stepped to one side to pass me, although the woman cast me one woeful backward look as they retreated.

To be charitable, perhaps they had been quarrelling about whether they would be able to see Schiehallion from the top. Maybe they'd come from a funeral, or had just discovered that there was to be another series of *Beadle's About*. To be uncharitable, perhaps they were just a pair of rude bastards, who should be slapped hard for not being polite enough to say hello to the only other human being for miles around.

It's always simple to find the path on the way down a hill, since you have the advantage of height, and so as I neatly avoided the boulder field I plodded down the track silently hoping that the couple had reached the summit of Ben More only to find they'd left their packed lunch in Perth.

On arriving back at the hotel I climbed into a bath and had a bit of a chat with myself before I lost the power of speech. At dinner I said 'thank you' three times, and

'Could I have a Becks please' once, before going to bed at 9.45.

If there's one thing lonelier than the wild hills of Scotland, it's the hotels.

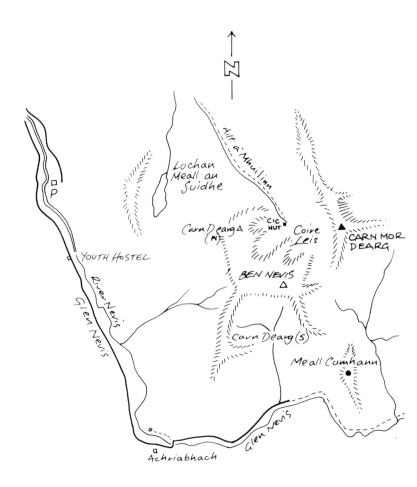

Carn Mor Dearg To Ben Nevis

Carn Mor Dearg; 1223m; (OS Sheet 41; 177722); M7.
Ben Nevis; 1344m; (OS Sheet 41; 166713); M1.

THE THOUGHT OF ASCENDING BEN NEVIS ON A Saturday filled me with dread. Not because it is difficult. Far from it. People, for reasons best known to themselves, regularly push wardrobes or pull pianos up the motorway that calls itself the tourist path. The only technical difficulty therefore is getting past those carrying a flat-pack fitted kitchen, or getting stuck on the path blocked by a group descending with an attractive Liberty-print sofa bed and a nest of tables.

The feature that makes it dreadful is that it is crammed with unattractive tourists throughout the summer months, shambling around 50 feet above sea level in a state of exhaustion, asking everyone if they're near the top yet. Perhaps it's mountain snobbery to wish to avoid such a crowd, and if so then I am a mountain snob. It's precious meeting the odd soul on a high top and passing the time of day with them, knowing that no matter who or what they are, you share the same interests in wildlife, wilderness and solitude. It's quite another thing to share a summit with 60 people who express disappointment that there is no hot-dog stand.

However, if those who successfully gain the top, with or without the burden of living-room furniture, feel blessed with the exhilaration and wonder of their surroundings then I am happy for them, and glad they are able to share an emotion I regularly enjoy on the hills. It's merely that if there's more than 50 of them feeling it simultaneously on the same summit then I'd rather be somewhere else.

But the Ben must be bagged, and happily it can be combined with the ascent of another massive Munro, Carn Mor Dearg, which will steer you away from the tourist path and into some grander territory.

Rashly, I chose a Saturday in early summer to pick off the two peaks. The Ben is quite a different place in winter, equally as magnificent, but free from Pac-o-macs, folding aluminium chairs, and people who want to know who Benjamin Nevis was and why the mountain is named after him. But once you have unfolded an ordnance survey map and made the cheese and pickle sandwiches, it's hard to change your mind, and so on a hot June day I set off up the zig-zagging tourist path from Glen Nevis at ten o'clock in the morning.

The path was built to serve an observatory that functioned at the top of the Ben at the turn of the century. One trusts that its astronomers weren't quite the size of Patrick Moore or getting to work could have been

problematic. Easy path or not, a climb of over 4,000 feet
every Monday morning would certainly make me phone
in with a headache. The track has been immaculately
maintained considering the pounding it takes from
trainers, brogues and sling-back stilettos, but being
Britain's highest peak has elevated Ben Nevis above
mere Munro status to major tourist attraction. A wooden
bench a short way up strewn with cigarette ends tells you
something about those who only make it that far, but
then the path is a long, steep ascent for anyone unused
to hill-walking.

To pass the heaving multitudes on the track, I raced
up like a fell runner, unhappily only to find each time
I successfully overtook what looked like a queue for an
Andrew Lloyd Webber musical that there were further
extensive crocodiles of people ahead. By this time I was
frothing at the mouth like a rabid dog in walking boots
with the effort of running in the heat, so I gave in and
resumed normal speed.

There is no course of action that will help you lose
the cacophony of teenagers yelling, adults whining and
children screaming, until the turn off for Carn Mor Dearg,
which joyfully appears at Lochan Meall an t-Suidhe.
It's advisable therefore to assume a sociable demeanour
and tolerate the company of your fellow man, rejoic-
ing in his plain humanity all over the path. The nice
beer-bellied English gentleman with the Union Jack
T-shirt and shorts, a can of lager in one hand and a
cigarette in the other, has just as much right to be
there as you do. He probably thinks you're a plonker
for carrying a rucksack and wearing hefty boots with

gaiters when the temperature is in the eighties. So smile, be charming, and resist the temptation to elbow small children off the path to their doom for the crime of carrying a ghetto-blaster up the hill.

From the lochan you turn north-east, back into some semblance of peace. A cairn marks the crossroads, and although the outrageously boggy path will cover you in peat to the armpits, you may hug yourself in delight to be walking in empty country again, as the cries of 'Look, Mam. Why is that man pushing a bed up the hill?' die behind you in the breeze.

However, beware of becoming overexcited that you are now on the path heading straight towards Carn Mor Dearg. It leads only to the Charles Inglis Clark mountain hut, a prestigious private hut owned by the Scottish Mountaineering Club and hence frequented by respectable rock-climbing doctors, lawyers and accountants. The hut is in a most peculiar situation, perched perfectly as the

Carn Mor Dearg

map would imply, to receive the maximum effect of the avalanche loading slopes behind it. Not only that, but one imagines such huts to be found in the very heart of the wilderness, where one cannot ascend a peak and walk out in a single day, and must take shelter for the night. Hardly the case here. A resident at the C.I.C. hut could easily do a spot of rock-climbing, nip into Fort William to indulge in some leisurely shopping for tartan gonks and still be back in time for a sing-song round the primus stove. Still, as long as the occupants are happy huddling in a spartan hut with the fantasy that they are men of the wilds, while people read the *Daily Record* under a golf umbrella and pass round the digestives a few thousand feet above them on the Ben, then who can criticize? Each to their own.

So the path must be abandoned here while you strike down to cross the Allt a' Mhuilinn and start a relentless slog to attain the ridge of Carn Mor Dearg. From down in the corrie, the first view appears of the Ben's mighty cliffs and the spectacular Carn Mor Dearg Arête, which must be crossed to link the two peaks. Don't imagine you can walk easily straight up on to the Arête from the bottom of the corrie, as you may get into difficulties near the top unless you've a head for heights. It may look easy from the safety of the burn's heathery banks, but you would be wringing out your underpants if you found yourself clinging to near-vertical rock at the crest of the ridge by pursuing such a daft route. There are of course one or two ways up the face of the Arête but personally I wouldn't advise it. And you would miss Carn Mor Dearg which, after the relentless pull to climb on to its broad back, rewards you with the most fabulous views, and an easy walk to its summit. From here the cliffs of Ben Nevis are at their most dramatic, a sight sadly denied to those who take the tourist path. They approach the Ben from its wide whale-backed side, and hence stand at the top of these cliffs without being able to view them.

As you stroll or stumble along the ridge, you are presented with a vista of deep gullies, rarely without snow, and terrifying chimneys slicing up through the rock. To the east are the Aonachs, the brooding big beasts tamed to a degree now by poor old Aonach Mor's ski-tows, which it wears uncomfortably like a lorry driver sporting gold neck chains.

It's tricky, as someone who skis and mountaineers, to whine about the encroachment of ski developments in Scotland, especially when the developers of Aonach Mor spilt so much ink about how they were 'conservation friendly', they could have made a major motion picture out of their press releases. Unfortunately, all the bleating in the world about being green can't conceal the fact that a previously wild, virgin hillside now resembles Gateshead. They run the Gondola in the summer months too, which provides an additional worry that groups of sweet little old ladies in overcoats, support tights and patent shoes, could find themselves wandering aimlessly on top of a mountain over 4,000 feet high, without any concept of the dangers.

The next danger for me was the Arête. Carn Mor Dearg's cairn provides a perfect view of the remaining route, with the Arête sweeping elegantly off to the south-west. To those of us with vertigo, it fortunately reveals that the southern side of the ridge is not nearly as precipitous as the northern. This, in plain terms, means that apart from one small section of scrambling, you can chicken out and walk along the Arête with your head bobbing safely below the crest.

Constantly at war with my vertigo, I decided not to be pathetic and strode off on the flat, step-like slabs that top the crest of the ridge. After a spot of scrambling below the summit of Carn Mor Dearg, the only intimidating section is at the other end, just below the boulder field that will take you on to the summit of the Ben.

Crampon marks on the ridge are a little disquieting. Not because you wonder if you need them in June, but because they are long white scars instead of neat little puncture marks. Call me suspicious, but this implies that the crampon, far from adhering steadily to the spot upon which its owner has chosen to commit his or her weight, has decided it prefers an altogether different rock and has gone for a bit of a slide. Written in stone all along the ridge therefore are visual records of people going 'Whoooaaargh!' with every step. This was not something upon which I wished to dwell, as I approached the narrowest section of the ridge. Being Saturday, there were a number of burly walkers picking their way over the granite from both directions which, unlike the presence of the bermuda-shorted brigade puffing their way up the other side of Ben Nevis, was curiously comforting.

As I gingerly stepped on to one last narrow slab, I met someone I knew walking the other way. Delightful as it was to meet pleasant company in such an unlikely place, I very badly wanted to exchange our felicitations on the other side of this rock. There, I felt, we could chat for hours without the fear of stepping back absentmindedly and continuing the conversation from a hospital bed in Fort William. He was having none of it, so I concealed my vertiginous anxieties.

We made some small talk as I tried to fix my eyes on his face to forget that my palms were sweating and my peripheral vision was registering only sky. The fact we were chatting about a programme on Radio 4 while standing on a dainty platform hundreds of feet tall seemed not to bother him. It was bothering me immensely. So I wrapped up the conversation as rudely as someone on *Newsnight* trying to silence a politician, just as he dealt me a social body blow. Would I mind taking his photo on this slab with the ridge spreading out behind him?

'Not at all,' said my mouth.

'LET ME OFF HERE!' screamed the rest of me.

So pressing his camera to my eye I tried to focus on this tanned, happy man, standing with one boot over the edge of a 200- or 300-foot drop, and the other on the edge of thin air. Who knows how the picture turned out? So prolific was my perspiration I steamed up the viewfinder, and I imagine my acquaintance now possesses a fine set of prints featuring the edge of my thumb and some clouds. We said our farewells and I leapt gratefully off the ridge and on to the safe path with the elegance of a stunned ox.

From here the last leg is a simple but muscle-tearing walk up a large boulder field to the summit of Ben Nevis. The posts stuck into the rock to your right as you ascend are markers for winter to stop people going off the edge; they also double as abseil posts for a quick escape route. There are those who think it rather offensive to erect such permanent climbing aids on a wild mountain, although we're not exactly talking a carved mahogany banister with brass handrails. It's also somewhat perverse to complain about a few innocent posts when the top of Ben Nevis is a lofty scrapyard.

Reaching the summit from the boulder field is a strange experience. From a steep ascent you emerge on to a surprisingly large plateau the size of a football field, covered with cairns, memorial plaques, the ruined observatory, and of course the people you left behind on the tourist path. The ruins of the observatory are of interest but the rest of the summit could do with a hoover. But if you ignore the commemorative debris and assortment of international litter you will enjoy the most exhilarating views that can include over 100 Munros when visibility is good.

I arrived breathless, to find a large crowd and a respectable covering of snow on the summit. The snow in June was a revelation which seemed to astonish and dismay some girls in bikini-tops with a cold-box full of beer and a shoulder bag full of Jackie Collins novels, who had clearly hoped to picnic at the top. Britain's highest peak is not to be taken lightly. Although mountaineers will not need reminded, the less experienced need to be constantly alerted to the fact that a hot, sunny car park does not necessarily mean a benign hill-walk. The summit may be, and more often than not is, like Ice Station Zebra. Never feel uncomfortable warning people you encounter halfway up a mountain who are dressed for the beach that they are taking a great risk proceeding without extra clothing and food. You may sound like a Victorian headmaster, but how much worse would you feel to read of those people being injured, lost or killed when you could have prevented it? So what if they tell you to sod off and mind your own business? At least your conscience will be clear.

Since nobody on the summit of the Ben required a ticking off, except perhaps by the fashion police, it was back on to the tourist path for the descent. Not only can you feel smug that you bagged the Ben the hard way, you will also be handsomely rewarded by the views across Loch Linnhe as you descend. Even depressed Fort William takes on a magnificence from this height as it glitters and reflects the late evening sun.

I avoided the mob on the path by descending 200 feet sledging on my rucksack on a long snow bank. I hasten to add before I am taken to court by mountain men with beards that this is highly irresponsible behaviour and extremely dangerous. Bloody good fun though. Safety pundits will be pleased to note that I received my just desserts that evening, on unpacking my rucksack and discovering that the action had mashed a forgotten egg sandwich into my hat.

The whole walk took in excess of nine hours, so not one to consider if you want to make it home in time for *Blind Date.* Don't let the volume of traffic discourage you from this superb walk. I was thrilled by it, delighted not only by the unsurpassed views in all directions, but by the physical challenge that a walk with so much climbing and descending presents. There is no denying that even in summer Ben Nevis is a magnificent peak, and a winter ascent for those well equipped and prepared will be a doubly stirring experience.

For those who wish to claim the peak with a selection of walnut dining-room furniture, try to avoid the hottest months of the year. Direct sunlight plays havoc with the varnish.

Rambler, Scrambler Or Dangler?

I'VE ALWAYS SAID I CLIMB MUNROS. EVERYONE I go climbing Munros with says they climb Munros. We phone each other and say, 'Do you want to go and climb a Munro tomorrow?' It seems a logical thing to say if you fancy climbing a Munro, but apparently we are living a lie. We don't climb Munros because we are not climbers. Now you might think that a little strange, after all the *Concise Oxford Dictionary* defines 'climb' thus: 'ascend, mount, go up (often with help of hands)'.

Yep, that just about sums up what we do on the way to the cairn, hence the use of the word climb in trying to convey to a companion exactly what it is you expect them to do when they get out of the car. We don't say we writhe with the Munros because we don't slither up them on our bellies, nor would we invite friends to hop, swim, float or jitterbug up a Munro on a Saturday. The term 'climb' has done us proud for years. The reason it is now unacceptable to say it is that at some point in recent history, rock-climbers held a secret annual general meeting and decided to keep the word to themselves. They climb, we merely walk.

Climbers also like to call themselves 'danglers'. This, I trust, has no connection with the fecal matter we are used to seeing hanging around the back end of a sheep, but instead refers to the fact they spend most of their weekends dangling from a rope.

The problem is that rock-climbers do all the hardest stuff in this game. Instead of meandering up a path to the top, chatting amicably to a pal about how George Michael used to be good in Wham and passing round the butterscotch, they choose a cliff and try to reach the summit by slowly inching their way up vertical rock, pushing their fingers into tiny fissures and standing with one toe on a ledge the size of a pebble. As you might imagine, this takes some time and is also completely mental. So on gaining the top, where the walkers are tucking into their second pork pie, the rock-climber needs some way to distinguish him or herself as greatly superior. This is hard. After all, the walkers got to the top first. The walkers have already had their lunch. The walkers still have some finger nails left and don't have skid marks in their boxer shorts. The rock-climber is powerless to inspire respect. But the revenge comes later in the pub.

Walker to rock-climber – 'So, were you out on the hill today?'

Rock-climber smiles sardonically, wiping his mouth with the back of a hairy arm. 'Yeah. Did an E7.'

Walker is confused. 'Oh. The Easains. Nice. A bit far away from Torridon though. Well we did Liathach. A lovely day's climb.'

Rock-climber chokes on beer. Splutters through ale-soaked beard. 'Climb? Climb did you say? You're talking walk in the park, matey! I mean I did a climb – A CLIMB! Comprende?'

Walker starts to regret starting conversation. Looks round for escape from this man who is obviously a few co-ordinates short of a bearing, and starts to back away slowly.

'Well, we certainly thought we were climbing, the wife and me, you know with all that pulling ourselves up over the rock and all, and what with the fact we were, well, in a manner of speaking, how can I put this, em, climbing up to the top.'

Rock-climber lunges at walker and tries to force-feed him his Yeti-gaiters until restrained.

A nasty, but not uncommon incident. So how can the simple walker make sure he avoids such an unpleasant confrontation with a dangler? Perhaps the most important lesson is to be able to recognize a rock-climber when you see one. Rock-climbers make sure they have lots of metal implements swinging from them at all times. This, I must confess, is quite sexy, in the same way that young, handsome joiners with their belt of tools strung low round their hips can make an impressionable adolescent girl want to have shelves erected. The rock-climber is held on a rope by clipping himself on to a harness thingy (if you've come to this book for technical information, boy are you going to be disappointed) that straps round his thighs and crotch, so as a quick guide to who the climbers are in the pub, just watch for those who seem to be constantly fiddling around in their genital area. I've noticed climbers do this a lot. They are always hitching up underpants, scratching away happily at unspeakable things in their breeches and, with one finger, boldly trying to free their underpants that have become lodged somewhere dark and irretrievable that we can only guess at. Before any girls get excited at the prospect of all these crotch-obsessed men packing out Glencoe bars, and rush off to join a climbing club, I should point out they also smell like a circus tarpaulin and regard ten pints of Guinness as an aperitif.

So if we must accept that these climbers, or danglers, are kings of the mountains, then who comes next in this rigid pecking order? It's the scramblers. I, apparently, am a scrambler. That means that in addition to walking up the hill with my hands in my pockets, sometimes I scramble up rocks using my hands. Kind of obvious really. I can't imagine I would try and scramble up over rocks using my nose, but the use of hands in the mountaineering hierarchy seems to be of prime importance. Scramblers probably make up the majority of Munro-baggers, since to do them all you can't avoid scrambling, and will also be obliged to dangle once on the Inaccessible Pinnacle on Skye. There's noticeably less equipment hanging from a scrambler, but pound for pound there will be more fleecy material visible. Climbers like to break away from the usual uniform of breeches and warm top, favouring instead old tracksuit bottoms and rancid T-shirts, but the scrambler usually likes to be well turned out. However, the easiest way to distinguish the two groups is that the walker/scrambler will stand at the bottom of a difficult and dangerous mountain looking for a safe and easy way up, and the

climber/dangler will stand at the foot of a safe and easy mountain looking for a difficult and dangerous way up.

Luckily for us scramblers, there is a group even further down the mountain social scale. They are known as ramblers. Unfortunately I am unable to advise you how to spot a rambler in pub, since ramblers don't go into pubs. They either brew up tea on a little gas stove beside their car, or pop into a coffee house for a bun and a flick through *The Observer Book of Birds*. Ramblers are keen on things like 'rights of way', even though everywhere in Scotland is a right of way to those who cause no damage. This is because quite a lot of them are English and can't see the difference between Knoydart and Chipping Sodbury. They will write pamphlets and go on protest marches to keep open a path running from a new Barrett housing estate through a farmer's potato field to a scrap yard on the banks of a canal. They seem like terribly nice people, concerned with wildlife, erosion, litter and rights of way through potato fields, but a dangler or scrambler caught in a confined space with a tenacious rambler will end up either committing an act of violence or huddling in a foetal position in the corner, dribbling saliva from a defeated face as the rambler concludes his theory about red deer numbers.

Mountain Rescue get little trouble from ramblers, since their rambles rarely take them off a bus route, and you can sometimes spot them at the sides of the road, gazing into a hedgerow as their leader tells them a little about the history of couch grass.

Climbers make a great mistake, however, in imagining that each of these groups aspires to the dizzy heights of dangling. This is not true. I don't want to rock-climb. Unlike a sport like skiing, the considerable risks are not matched with sufficient exhilaration to kindle my interest, although I wouldn't say no if a boyfriend were to slip naked into one of those clanking climbing harnesses after a hot bath and a glass of wine.

Neither do ramblers wish to scramble. They are happy rooting around for Fly Agaric toadstools in a farmer's back garden until he sets the dogs on them, and would be miserable if you dragged them up anything taller than a caravan.

What is in dispute is who is allowed to say they went climbing. I shall carry on using the term regardless, and any hairy man who wants to challenge me about it is welcome to a wrestle. As long as he wears his harness.

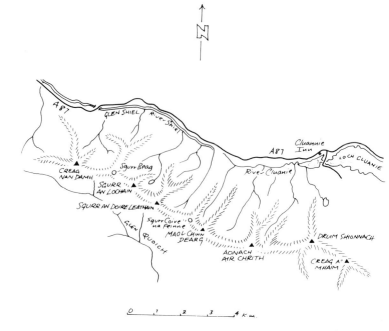

The South Glen Shiel Ridge

Creag a' Mhaim; 947m; (OS Sheet 33; 088078); M214.
Druim Shionnach; 987m; (OS Sheet 33; 074085); M155.
Aonach air Chrith; 1021m; (OS Sheet 33; 051083); M107.
Maol Chinn-dearg; 981m; (OS Sheet 33; 032088); M166.
Sgurr an Doire Leathain; 1010m;
(OS Sheet 33; 015099); M116.
Sgurr an Lochain; 1004m; (OS Sheet 33; 005104); M126.
Creag nan Damh; 918m; (OS Sheet 33; 983112); M268.

EVEN THE MOST DEDICATED MUNROIST CAN BE side-tracked by the wicked pleasures of city life. The temptation to stay in town for a curry or a Schwarzenegger film, or both, can seriously disrupt that urge to carry on the journey up the 277 summits.

You can spot the symptoms of Munro fatigue immediately. Gradually a long lie on a Saturday comes to mean rising at 5 p.m. in time for the *Brookside* omnibus, your rucksack quietly grows grey mouldy bits at the back of a dark cupboard, and *The Face* seems more interesting than Tom Weir's 'My Month'. It's healthy, of course, to have more than one burning interest in life, but weekends are precious. To waste them cleaning out a drawer of plastic carrier bags instead of scrambling up lofty pinnacles is something you may regret. So should you discover that you are spending more time in Safeways than on the north-bound carriageway of the A9, it's time to tackle the South Glen Shiel Ridge.

In a single day, without leaving the ridge, a fit walker can pick off seven Munros and stagger back home to an orgy of peak-ticking at the back of the Munro book. There's no better inspiration for shrugging off slothfulness than Glen Shiel, which rewards with such a high score of tops and something worthwhile to brag about to those who spent Saturday and Sunday vacuuming the car with a cordless hoover.

The ideal place to start this heavenly 14-kilometre trek is from the equally lovely Cluanie Inn, a hotel at the western end of Loch Cluanie. I spent two nights there one summer, giving myself the immeasurable luxury of being able to start early from the hotel, still burping porridge and bacon, and return to a hot dinner, a steaming bath and a cosy bar full of fellow hill-walkers. You can camp nearby and use the Cluanie Inn for a hot bar-meal and somewhere to consume beer beside a log fire until they throw you out, but if you have the money why deny yourself a bed for the night?

The Cluanie Inn is a fine hotel in a splendid old building, which has been extended in recent years so sensitively, soon it will be difficult for passers-by to tell the old from the new. The new accommodation is on one floor, set round a pretty courtyard which echoes the traditional details of the existing structure. Of course this kind of thoughtful extension is alien to most Highland hotel owners. Their mission in life appears to be competing with one another in a race to remould their ancient and historic rural buildings into approximations of Birmingham town centre. If only such offenders were punished by having a Radio One DJ surgically joined to them at the hip, perhaps they would understand the crime of incongruous and pig-ugly extensions.

It's a stroke of great fortune that the Cluanie Inn's proprietors are more enlightened, since the building dominates the eastern end of the glen. As you wander along the ridge, it's a long time before you lose sight of its neat white contours, and if you take a strong pair of binoculars on your walk, you can keep an eye on how the housemaid is turning your bed down.

A long ridge-walk requires an early start, and a companion and I set off from the hotel at 8.30, toast crumbs still trembling on our lips, to attain the ridge by the first peak, Creag a' Mhaim. It's an easy walk up a tarmac estate road to the south-east of the hotel, which gently gains height until it's time to strike up the hillside towards Munro number one. There is no conspicuous path, but in fine weather the route could not be more obvious.

I had looked forward to a leisurely ramble amongst the hills, since we had started early and the days were long. But as we left the tarmac road and headed up the hill I made a grave error. We came across a small party of people sitting innocently on a rock enjoying the sunshine. Obviously they had risen even earlier. They said hello cheerily as we passed, and for no particular reason other than mindless banter I concluded our exchange with some hopeless attempt at humour, which happily has been blacked from my memory. I recall the gist of it implied that they couldn't sit there sunbathing too long if they wanted to get through all seven tops. Not exactly side-splitting, but not grounds for assault either, one would think. One of the men visibly bristled as the others smiled their pleasant responses. The race was on.

Although ten full minutes passed after leaving his party swigging juice happily and pointing at the loch, a casual glance backwards revealed that they were gaining on us quickly. This was very strange. To have closed such a gap the niggled gentleman must have swiped the juice from his companions' lips the moment we passed and kick-started them into a sprint. It may be a childish response, but when you have overtaken someone on a hill, it is very uncomfortable to be overtaken by them. We stepped up the pace. So did they.

The ridge is quickly gained and on this peach of a day was absolutely magnificent, with the hills retaining sizeable patches of spring snow that sparkled in the hazy sunshine. Although there are no technical difficulties on this walk, the ridge rarely disappoints, and the terrain varies from narrow, dramatic sections that thrill with their mantle of cliffs, to huge grassy plains pitted with tiny alpine flowers.

The ridge presents its craggy face to the north and rolls away in steep, but somewhat tamer, banks to the south. Unlike a ridge like the Aonach Eagach where escape is impossible until the end, it is not only feasible, but very tempting to come off the ridge and wander into the wild land of the Glenquoich forest that appears so inviting from the tops. On a summer's day, the sun glitters on Loch Quoich, back-lighting the lonely bridge that takes a single track road to the remote Kinloch Hourn. You can just make it out as you cross from Aonach air Chrith to Maol Chinn-dearg, with Loch Quoich sparkling behind Gleouraich, another fabulous mountain.

Slicing through Gleouraich's slopes are some incredibly well-constructed stalkers' paths. My heart sank when I first viewed them, since huge paths marching across wild hills usually signal the coming of insensitive forestry. But I was comforted to discover that these highways are antiquities, built by some unfortunate landowner who expected a visit from the king. The king never turned up and the laird was left with paths on which he could hold a formula one race. I say unfortunate laird, but of course it would have been the unfortunate estate workers who would have hauled the pick-axes up the hill and toiled away for weeks, just so that somebody with a crown could sit on a pony that didn't stumble on his way up a mountain to shoot something. Hard to feel sorry for the laird, who would have watched the sweating workers from his window, hands in pockets, listening for the doorbell in case the king changed his mind and dropped in for a scone.

We completed the first four Munros with relative ease, since there is little rising or dropping between peaks, and cruised along a gloriously flat section of the ridge having fantasies about lunch. There were a number of

Looking east along t

uth Glen Shiel Ridge

walkers now, all taking their time and drinking in the
view, but the chap at our heels had now resorted to
breaking away from his party to try and close the gap
so obviously gnawing at his soul. I had never done
anything as crass as race on a hill-walk before, but it
was starting to amuse. Although it hardly seemed fair
racing a man at least 15 years our senior, who could
resist going just a little faster every time we saw his face
contorted with exertion, glaring up at us like Charles
Laughton in *Mutiny On The Bounty*?

A lunch break would give him his chance, forcing
him to make a decision whether or not to delay his own
sustenance in order to overtake us as we crammed fruit
cake into our faces. We decided to halt the nonsense and
stopped for a sandwich on a picturesque rocky outcrop
that provided views east and west along the glen, and
over to spectacular Knoydart. The running man took his
opportunity, and as he passed, followed by his less com-
petitive, wheezing companions, clearly suffering agonies
by his pace-setting, he gave us a triumphant, knowing
nod.

What is more enjoyable than silently consuming
chicken sandwiches surrounded by scenery that immobi-
lizes any other emotion but wonder? Once gained, the
ridge never disappoints. The best route is east to west, as
following the sun results in the treat of trying to glimpse
the sea and watching the sun set. It brings a hazard too.
Even though the wind kept the tops cool, the sun was
relentless, and I foolishly changed out of my breeches into
shorts for the remainder of the route. I wonder when I
will learn that on a long walk in a single unchanging

direction, one will automatically go home with a left leg sporting first-degree burns and a right limb like a piece of white Italian veal? However, elation at the beauty of the surroundings meant tandooried legs were far from my thoughts, and as we continued to the shapely Sgurr an Lochain, towering as it does over a tiny dark blue lochan, we agreed it couldn't get much better.

Although there is no mention of it on the map, I could swear that the tiny loch has a crannog in it. I'm sure archaeologists will rush to correct me but, from the vantage point high above it, there does seem to be a suggestion of a circular structure beneath the water, joined to the banks by a walkway. If it is a crannog, it's in a strange place, stuck high above the glen in a corrie. It would have taken its occupants hours to get to the Cluanie Inn for a pint from there.

Just as we stepped over a rise, we nearly fell over the boy racer and party having their lunch. The others acknowledged us cheerily, clearly relieved to have been allowed 30 seconds for a sit-down. He looked catatonic with rage. As we parted, we could hear our man force-feeding his companions their scotch eggs, hurrying them along like a rowing cox.

He didn't catch us until the last peak, Creag nan Damh, where a number of ridge-walkers were gathered, basking in the delight of the afternoon and resting on their laurels after a mammoth expedition. If you had any energy at all, you could keep height and continue to Sgurr na Sgine and on to The Saddle, but you would need thighs like Graeme Souness's. It's here you come to realize three things. 1. The South Glen Shiel Ridge

is fabulous. 2. You have seven miles to walk back to the hotel as you haven't got two cars. 3. You're knackered. Very gingerly, everybody started to question each other about transport. No, nobody had left a car at the bottom of this hill, and, yes, everybody was looking to cadge a lift.

By this time our pursuer had joined the merry band on the peak, and we could hear his companions gasping not far behind him. We had beaten him, but he played a final trump card. He had two cars. They were at the bottom of the hill. He was going back to the Cluanie Inn. Yes, there was probably room for us all.

Normally, walking along tarmac is a piece of cake after the rocky excursion along a ridge. But in summer the A87 is crammed with caravan-dragging buffoons who drive as though wearing strait-jackets. The choice for the pedestrian is either a leap into the ditch for safety, or a nasty death smeared over their ridiculous tin box like a dripping red caravan-club sticker. There was nothing else for it. It was time to give in and do a bit of grovelling.

All the way down we listened with feigned interest to our man's proud record of clock-beating on other hills. We tolerated his hilarious English mispronunciations of the Scottish hills that had taken him less than three hours, keeping in mind the thought of that comfortable car seat at the bottom of this rough heather slope every time we felt like killing him. At last we arrived at his car, where several other walkers were hanging around looking dolefully along the road.

I couldn't do it. I just couldn't take a journey in a confined space with a man who pronounced Sgurr na

Ciste Duibhe as Sisty Dub and didn't think this was as good as the Lake District.

Just as this realization dawned, a luckless couple drew into the parking space to read a map. Before they knew what was happening we had opened their door, asked for a lift, said thank you and got in. A good tip in hitching is to approach your intended lift when stationary. It's practically impossible to say no to someone who's actually loaded their rucksack into your boot and clipped on their seatbelt. With little choice they drove us sullenly to the hotel. As you drive, or walk, God forbid, back along the road, it's hard to believe you have travelled all that way at a lofty 3,000 feet. The ridge seems massive from the road, and when we tried to tell our driver where we'd been, he grunted in disbelief. Well it may have been a grunt of irritation that his lovely hire-car was steaming up with two sweaty, stinking hill-walkers who had forced their way in uninvited, but I prefer to think disbelief.

The cold pint at the Cluanie Inn was nectar and, as we polished it off, our man and his party arrived. Not only had we beaten him on the ridge, but without cars we had unwittingly beaten him back to the hotel. The walkers who had wangled the lift with him looked as if they had been told they had a week to live, suggesting the car conversation must have fulfilled my expectations.

We bought him and his friends a drink which gave him a chance to quiz us on our movements for the next day. My companion's eyes glittered impishly as he said we would be combining The Five Sisters with The Saddle and Sgurr na Sgine, hoping to be finished by 5 p.m.

'It'll take an early start,' he said.

We retired to a hot bath and glimpsed them only briefly over a sweet trolley later at dinner. The next morning was drizzling, damp and miserable and our man and his party were not at breakfast.

'You're not first up this morning,' said the waiter. 'That other lot left at 6.30 to do The Five Sisters and The Saddle.'

We ate a leisurely breakfast and then drove to Skye to have some scones.

Creag Meagaidh

Creag Meagaidh; 1130m; (OS Sheets 34 and 42; 418875);
M26.

SOMETIMES EVEN THE EASIEST OF MOUNTAINS CAN
defeat you. There is nothing particularly difficult about
Creag Meagaidh, unless it comes up in a spelling test,
yet it took me three attempts to get to the top of the
damned thing.

It's only in recent years that I've learned to use
the weather forecast before contemplating a hill-walk.
Millions of pounds spent on satellite technology is wasted
when people like me ignore Michael Fish yelling on
television from behind some sandbags, 'For God's sake
take cover!' as we set off to claim a Munro with a song
in our hearts.

It was just such foolhardy behaviour that enabled
me continually to miss the summit of Creag Meagaidh.
The first attempt was in winter, precisely at that dark,

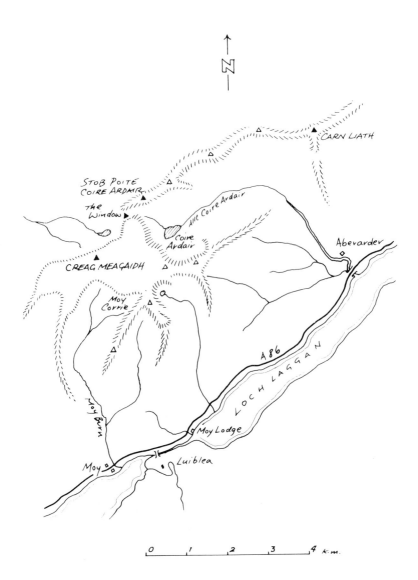

N

CARN LIATH

STOB POITE
COIRE ARDAIR

The
Window

Allt Coire Ardair

Coire
Ardair

Aberarder

CREAG MEAGAIDH

Moy
Corrie

A 86

LOCH LAGGAN

Moy Burn

Moy Lodge

Moy   Luiblea

0   1   2   3   4 km.

depressing period when the sun can barely be bothered rising for more than 20 minutes before it packs in and hands over to nightfall. The weather on this occasion seemed ideal. A heavy snowfall left the hills deliciously inviting and the sky was clear and bright.

Two of us set off up the long path from Aberarder at the mind-bogglingly stupid time of 11.30 a.m. In the mists of time I cannot recall why we started so late. Perhaps there was a party the night before, maybe we hung around in bed too long doing most wicked things, or more likely I just slept in. Whatever the excuse, we reached Lochan a' Choire at 3 p.m. when the sun was starting to remember it was needed elsewhere. Simple arithmetic told us that even if we gained the summit we would be stumbling back down in the dark like late cinema-goers trying to find their seats.

As we sat at the loch eating a cold lunch, deciding who could first pin the blame on the other for messing up the day, we heard voices from the cliffs surrounding the lochan. A third of the way up a vicious-looking ice-climb were two men, slowly hacking an unenviable route with axes and crampons. By this time it was past 3.30, the light was fading fast, and the blizzard that the ignored weatherman had warned would sweep the Highlands was whipping into action. That's odd, we thought. Perhaps they're going to spend the night on the mountain. Maybe they're top mountaineers training for a Himalayan expedition that requires constant overnight bivvying on icy rock faces. So we ignored them and went home. Unfortunately they turned out to be two fools who didn't realize the time, and brought Mountain Rescue out combing the hill for them next morning. Luckily, they had survival gear and were found alive and well, albeit a trifle sheepish, at the top of the climb.

I felt rather guilty after that episode. When should you tell Mountain Rescue that you think there might be somebody in danger? After all, if those two boys had died, it would have been on our consciences that we saw them get into difficulty and did nothing. On the other hand, imagine the embarrassment of calling a full-scale search out for somebody who is not only not in peril, but is mightily cheesed off to be awoken from a deep sleep by an RAF Sea-King helicopter blowing the filling out of their sleeping-bag? Not to mention the danger you put the members of the Mountain Rescue team in by expecting them to stagger about in the snow with sticks when they should be back home with their slippers on watching *McGregor's Scotland.*

I feel the same way about the police. When two men tried to break into my kitchen via a skylight window at midnight while I was at home, I made the grave error of dialling 999. Not only did the street fill with sirens and blue lights like an episode of *Kojak,* the cops that piled up the stairs were too fat to get through the attic space and pursue the men. That left me with dozens of portly gentlemen in blue who spent the rest of the night eating my shortbread, drinking my coffee and asking me if I knew Terry Wogan. Next time I will simply invite the burglars in. I'm certain they at least would refuse a second slice of cake.

Even though the plight of those two climbers should have released me from my fear of calling for help on behalf of others, I'm still wary unless I come across someone whose legs are a few hundred yards from their body. Reminding others that they don't have much light left, or are not equipped for the top, is quite different. But I live in fear of calling out the rescue team for a solitary figure glimpsed high on a darkening summit, only to find it's Hamish McInnes nipping back up to fetch a dropped mitten.

That was the first attempt at Creag Meagaidh. The second, on a blustery Sunday in October, was more frustrating. Ignoring the weather forecast yet again, a number of us packed our rucksacks and headed up that interminable path to Coire Ardair. Meanwhile, canny Munroists who paid attention to satellite technology, which indicated a depression deeper than Christmas in Barlinnie, were sitting at home by the fire eating cheese on toast. We should have taken some heed from the birch trees halfway up the track which were bending double in the gale, and from the fact that five minutes after leaving the car, we were wetter than the Scottish Sub-Aqua team. This, however, was a determined pack and we were not going to be put off by small obstacles like being unable to stand up or walk forward. This time I at least got past the lochan and up on to the boulder field that leads to the window. The window is a coll neatly dividing Creag Meagaidh and another Munro, Stob Poite Coire Ardair but, more significantly, it acts as a highly efficient wind tunnel. As we lurched up the soaking, slimy boulders towards it, like a team of wet-look mime artists walking against the wind, one of our party stopped and said, 'Let's go back.'

At least we all hoped that's what he said. In the gale it sounded like, 'Ehh . . . oaaah . . . aaaack.'

We were back in the car with the heater on before you could say 'Who finished the soup?' and another attempt was foiled.

The last failure was human. I made the mistake of telling two non-hill-walking friends that they could easily manage Creag Meagaidh. The day was perfect. A crisp winter morning greeted us with snow quilted in twinkling ice crystals. The time was 9 a.m., the sky was clear and blue, and nothing was going to stop me this time. What I failed to realize was that to those who never walk up mountains, visiting the bank, the post office and the dry cleaners on the same day is considered a triathlon.

My friends had to have their first sit-down in sight of the car. I was heartbroken. By 12.30 we had just made the birch wood and had to admit defeat. Friendship is more important than mountaineering, and so for their sakes I told them they'd done very well and we turned back to the prospect of a more leisurely Sunday afternoon, with colour supplements, cats, coffee and carpets to lie on. I cast one longing glance up at the cliffs of Coire Ardair, where the sun was glancing off the icy tips of gleaming rock, and I knew that next time I'd get the sucker.

It was therefore with a fit companion that I tackled the brute for a fourth attempt. This time we planned to take in two other Munros on the northern ridge of the corrie, Carn Liath and Stob Poite Coire Ardair, before dropping down to the window and back up on to Creag Meagaidh's vast plateau.

It was an amazing frosty morning, with a strange, silent mist hanging only a few hundred feet high. My heart sank at the prospect of yet again missing the top in the thick fog, but we had a great treat in store. We left the path, shrouded in a beautiful and eerie veil of mist, coloured pink with the rising sun, and clambered up the hillside towards the ridge of Carn Liath. My friend was about 50 feet above me and almost out of sight in the fog, when I heard him yell at me to 'come and see this'. Those who have never been up a mountain when temperature inversion is at work have missed the most splendid sight. We were standing above the clouds, which formed a thick, bulbous ocean at our feet, out of which in every direction rose mountain tops like islands. The mist was breaking against the peaks like waves, the sun was radiant in a perfectly clear blue sky above us, and I was awe-struck.

The Window, Creag Meagaidh

(See colour picture section) Ahead of us we could see our ridge, standing clear of the cloud, and blushed purple in the strange early light. The ridge-walk was one of the most wonderful I can recall, as the sea of cloud broke up only on gaining the Creag Meagaidh plateau, and the day remained crystal clear until the last.

Some may find the summit of Creag Meagaidh a little disappointing after the drama of its cliffs and corrie. The top is not visible from the road, and were it not for a sizeable cairn you could miss it altogether. The plateau is huge, flat and featureless, and tests the map-reading ability of those who arrive in anything but perfect visibility. A common error is to think that the large cairn first encountered when gaining the plateau from the window is the true summit. It is in fact something called Mad Meg's Cairn and nobody knows what the hell it's doing there. The Nature Conservancy Council, who thankfully own Creag Meagaidh, have a couple of suggestions, including it being a monument to a lost lover or an old protection for a rowan tree. Gardeners amongst you will doubtless argue that piling a ton and a half of rubble on top of your sapling is a somewhat off-beat method of protection, so I'll take the old lost love yarn, thanks.

I'm pleased the NCC bought the mountain, since a commercial forestry firm had plans to cover the whole area in vile rows of sitka spruces to help chat-show hosts and snooker players in England make a killing on their tax bills. Thankfully it's now a nature reserve, which has the added advantage of offering free access during the stalking season.

After so many attempts, that day could not have been more rewarding, and I've since been back at its summit twice. So don't let bad weather discourage you from claiming a targeted peak. It's not a defeat to turn back and return on a better day. You can look forward to some sort of a view and, let's face it, the mountain will still be there when you come back. That is unless it's sold to the sort of person who blasts half of his land away to quarry gravel for motorways, like someone I can think of on the west coast. If he buys your Munro, best get it bagged before the deeds change hands.

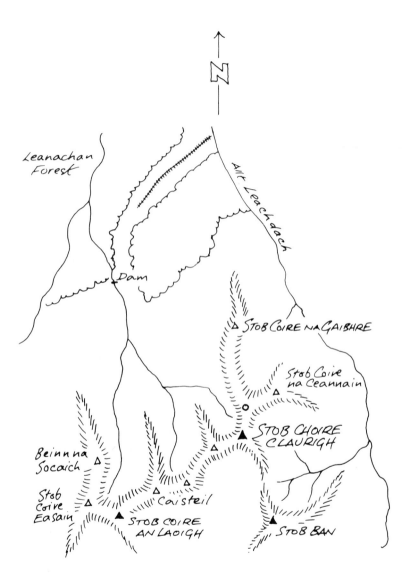

The Grey Corries

Stob Choire Claurigh; 1177m; (OS Sheet 41; 262739); M14.
Stob Coire an Laoigh; 1115m; (OS Sheet 41; 240725); M37.

I HAVE A PHOBIA ABOUT BEING CAUGHT DRIVING MY car on a private road, although I have no idea where this unreasonable fear emanates from. Perhaps when pregnant with me, my mother was hit on the head by a 'No Vehicular Access' sign, and her understandable anxiety transmitted itself to my foetal subconscious. One day I will pluck up the courage to quiz her. In the meantime I must live with the fact that I sweat like a *Sun* reader at a philosophy lecture every time my wheels crunch over someone else's gravel.

For this reason I was apprehensive about the approach to The Grey Corries, a fine ridge-walk to the south of Spean Bridge. The Scottish Mountaineering Club's Munros book mentioned a private road that 'at the time of writing' no objection was made to vehicles being taken along to the base of the walk. British Aluminium own the land, and, as soon as I realized I would have to trespass with a car, my imagination started its fevered travail. I would drive a few yards through the gate marked 'private' and instantly be set upon by men wielding knobbly aluminium clubs, or I would return from the walk to find my car had been smelted into a set of folding tubular garden furniture.

There was only one thing for it. Go in someone else's car. All I could offer was a hatchback whose tyres puncture as soon as it catches sight of anything other than motorway. My friend, however, possessed a Toyota Hilux four-wheel-drive pick-up truck, and there can be no better vehicle in which to trespass than one that looks as if it would get your daughter pregnant and drink all your beer. A feeble little hatchback in the Highlands deserves to be towed away. After all, when have you seen a hatchback contain anything other than daft city folk 'out for a run'? At least country bods use pick-ups to carry dung and move sheep. With the pick-up truck, if we learned to smoke roll-ups and wore denim jackets over our fleecy tops, we might be mistaken for locals.

We set out from Spean Bridge, where numerous coach parties enjoy real Highland hospitality in the Little Chef, before choosing from a rich selection of tartan travel rugs and heather-perfumed candles in the gift shop, and chugged our way up past Corriechoille farm.

Nobody stormed us with pitch forks, or even shouted 'hoi, you', as we opened and closed gates along the private section of road. My fears were unfounded. After such victory, an annoying revelation was that the starting point was crammed with hatchbacks, unquestionably owned by people who would never share my trepidation. The temptation to park on top of them rather than beside them was overwhelming, but then jacked-up pick-ups do that to you. Instead, we left the truck conventionally positioned, and headed up through the forest leading to the slopes of the first top, Stob Coire na Ceannain.

The grassy hillside steering you up on to the ridge starts off as a benign little stroll, until you realize it is going to continue forever. In the time it takes to get the better of this slope, you could raise a family and marry them off. Keeping a constant muscle-tearing gradient, there is no pity until the very top, and on such slopes it is handy to have a prop to allow yourself resting time. A camera can do the trick, letting you catch your breath before your lungs explode through your chest like *The Alien,* as you pretend to take a photo of an interesting stone. A change of clothing also lets you off the hook. Simply take something off or put something on, and your companion will never know the real reason you stopped. He or she will be obliged to wait politely as you go about your task, which you can time to complete at the same moment you recover the skill of breathing in and out.

At least at the top of this incline is a sight that makes the work worthwhile. Without warning, you emerge over a crest and stand before the magnificent grey scree, Coire na Ceannain, sweeping round a circular lochan that nestles in its lap. The relief of reaching the ridge is only matched by the excitement of the view. As you walk up to the first Munro, Stob Choire Claurigh, the whole complexity of the Aonachs becomes clear. This was a joy for me

as I had puzzled often on the jumble of tops visible from the A82 and in the mass of high peaks this area contains. The Grey Corries ridge offers an uncomplicated viewpoint. The vista is superb, presenting the fertile, genial great glen and Loch Lochy to the north, and the wild Mamore forest to the south, lurking behind pointy Stob Ban, a delicious little peak. This has to be one of my favourite mountain areas because of its variety and scale, and amazing accessibility from Glasgow and Edinburgh.

Despite the ominous row of trespassing hatchbacks, we saw nobody on the ridge at all, and luxuriated in the surprising solitude that one shouldn't expect so near a town like Fort William, which grows more like a Highland Gorbals every day. As a spotty student, I worked in a large hotel in Fort William for four months, and grew extremely fond of it. But I still retain sympathy for the misguided foreign tourists who read about its properties as a 'gateway to the beautiful western Highlands' and end up wandering in dismay down streets that make the Bronx look like Disneyland. After a couple of abortive attempts to reach the side of Loch Linnhe through dismal, litter-strewn lanes, over car parks and a dual carriageway, they return to abhorrent 60s concrete abominations masquerading as hotels. There, they presumably drink themselves into a stupor on black PVC bar stools before the coach comes and takes them somewhere even worse, like Aviemore. Fort William has its charms, like a couple of good supermarkets, a fascinating hardware shop, a fine shinty team and a great Indian restaurant. But in a contest to offer old rustic Scots charm, East Kilbride would beat it into the final.

However, urban squalor was not high on our list of topics as we picked off the last Munro, Stob Coire an Laoigh, oddly not marked on the ordnance survey map. From here you should descend along a northerly spur that will include two further tops, Stob Coire Easain and Beinn na Soacaich, and head for a dam, which you will find where the Allt Coire an Eoin meets the trees.

The dam is in a heavenly spot, situated at the end of a steep gorge, where the river above it tumbles down in a series of delightful waterfalls. The obvious thing to do is strip off and dive into the clear, green water, but I wouldn't advise it. Apart from being cold enough to remove your skin, there is a sinister tunnel sweeping water away on some underground journey, and although a metal grid may stop you from joining it, I have visions of diving in naked with a happy yell, only to emerge in the urinals of the aluminium smelter in Fort William. Besides which, on our visit we were rather discouraged from bathing by the sight of a dead lamb lying innocently at the bottom of the pool. Just imagine jumping in and putting your feet through it.

From here there is a path back to the car along a disused tramway. This is a thrilling construction, and if you fancy an interesting low-level walk you can follow it all the way from the Aonach Mor ski-area car park, through the Leanachan forest to the start point for The Grey Corries. It's a narrow rail that sometimes disappears altogether into rough path, and occasionally delights with perfectly intact Indiana Jones-style bridges over gulleys. Although warning signs shout at you not to cross these fragile constructions, as you're bound to fall off and die and don't say they didn't tell you so, you'd have to be a boring old git not to want to do a balancing act over them for thrills. However there's not too many of them from the dam as the section back to the car park is a tame ramble running through a clearing in the trees. We unfortunately missed it, and returned by the longer forest road, although a small compensation is the view looking back of Stob Coire an Laoigh framed perfectly by the pines. It's always essential to view the ridge you've just conquered, for the serious purpose of hugging yourself with glee, and a wonderful view of The Grey Corries can be savoured from the war memorial on the A82 north of Spean Bridge.

Another wonderful view was the truck, showing no signs of having been surrounded by angry aluminium workers attempting to tow it away. So it was an immediate retreat to Fort William for celebratory pakora and a chicken breast curry, where I changed out of my walking gear into some jeans to look like a local. Yes, I thought, they've seen me get out of the pick-up truck, I look wind-blown and ruddy, there's mud on my hands, they're bound to think I'm a crofter's wife.

The waitress approached.

'If that's your Capri outside you'd better watch and not get a ticket. It's a double yellow. Any side dishes with your curry?'

Cutting A Dash

IF YOU INTEND TO ESCAPE FROM THE TEEMING folly of city life and hightail it to the freedom of the hills, does it really matter what you wear? Of course it matters. You might think you're safe nipping out for a hill-walk in a Parka with nylon fur round the hood, and a pair of trawlerman's oilskin trousers you bought at a life-boat fund-raising stall, but that's the day you'll bump into Sean Connery and Christopher Lambert with a film crew making *Highlander 3*. If you're a male reader, you can reverse this law of probability, and be sure that you will meet Madonna doing a nude shoot for the Pirelli calendar on Ben Vorlich.

Unlikely as it seems, mountain vanity is rife. It's not enough any more to have comfortable boots and something waterproof to slip over a jumper. Your attire must tell other walkers and climbers how serious you are, indicate the status you enjoy in the world of mountaineering, and not make locals in the mountain's nearest bar fall dangerously silent when you pop in for a pint on the way back home.

For instance, let's take grey anoraks. The lust for grey anoraks is a profound sickness. The garments are usually shapeless, not very waterproof, and can be worn only with an olive-green acrylic hat, long, brown woollen slacks, and a pair of stout shoes from British Home Stores. Displayed in this manner, the grey anorak will serve its purchaser well, by having him ordered off the hill by Mountain Rescue before his car boot is slammed shut. If the owner is unfortunate enough to have a fall, the grey anorak will help him resemble a large rock when the RAF hover above, thus rendering him practically invisible. One can only assume that the purchasers of these lichen-grey accoutrements are members of EXIT, and that anyone attempting to rescue them would receive a bloody nose for their trouble. What other explanation could there possibly be for going into a shop, flicking through rails of attractive fuchsia, cobalt and aquamarine outer-garments, and saying to the assistant, 'Have you got any grey ones?'

Perhaps the shopkeeper should have a panic button under the counter to press during such a confrontation, and while humoring the shopper by pretending to go and look for some grey ones, stout men could rush in and restrain the customer before he can make it to his Access card. It's not as if grey anoraks are cheap. Since they are hard to find, except in odd little shops that specialize in big underpants for old people and sheepskin slippers, they cost a pretty penny. A certain firm famous for their 'bags' trouser suits, used to do an extensive line of grey anoraks, but they obviously had a visit from the style police and were made to put bits of navy blue and red in them or face a lengthy jail sentence. Not exactly Jean Paul Gaultier, but it's a start.

Of course it's possible to go too far the other way, a natural but perilous reaction to grey anorak anxiety, in fact a sort of anoraksia nervosa. Such hill-walkers are uncomfortable unless they look like the remnants box in an Indian wedding-sari shop. Every item of clothing, down to their underwear, is in designer day-glo and vibrant clashing tincture. They will happily walk about in the drizzle with a pink ice-axe, lime-green gaiters, a purple, yellow and turquoise rucksack, blue and orange kagoul, red breeches and a hat with the Union Jack on it. It's one thing to be seen on the hill, but quite another to be seen and have other climbers throw rocks at you.

I, sadly, am not blameless. If there were bouncers on mountains I would have been refused entry to the crags on more occasions than I care to recall. It's the inappropriate nature of my clothing that has consistently let me down through the years. I've already revealed that I started out in a donkey jacket, but I should add that it took me at least ten years to get a decent kit. A friend knitted me a fabulous Nordic jumper, which immediately took on the status of security blanket. During heat waves, companions walked beside me in shorts and a T-shirt, while I lurched along in two tons of wool, certain in the knowledge that removing the jumper for 30 seconds would result in instant death by exposure.

My boots were three sizes too big for me, since the man in the shop had convinced me it was necessary. I know now he was just trying to make a sale and didn't have

my size in stock, but since he was wearing a fleecy top
and tracksuit trousers I believed him, and bought these
huge leather edifices that a young married couple could
quite comfortably live in and bring up a family. This
meant that not only did the boots weigh more than a
small car, but I was obliged to wear four pairs of socks
to stop my feet moving about in them and turning my
heels into chilli con carne. You should always be very
careful when dealing with persuasive equipment sales
people. If I'd stayed any longer with the villain who
sold me those QE2 boots, I'd have walked from the shop
with a case of tent pegs and a canoe.

As Christmas and birthdays brought more Gortex, my
confidence grew and developed into mild snootiness about
people who didn't wear the right things on the hill. I
would tut at people trying to climb in wellingtons, and
roll my eyes at those in jeans. Didn't they realize that
mountaineering was a serious business? I certainly did,
and I had the magenta bum-bag to prove it.

Of course I was due for a humiliation. A friend and I
were driving in spring to Crarae gardens near Inveraray
so I could salivate over the rhododendrons, but we grew
tired of travelling at seven miles an hour behind clods
in caravans and on reaching the Rest And Be Thankful
pulled into the side to wander about at the base of Beinn
an Lochain. This is an interesting mountain, previously
a Munro, but had its stripes ripped off when the tables
were cruelly revised with more accurate measurements.
Since I was wearing posh garden visiting attire – a pair
of thin striped leggings, white leather ballet pumps,
a halterneck top, a cute bolero cardigan and dangly

earrings – we were only planning to leave the car for some air. However, we climbed up a little way, just to get off the road. Then we thought we should nip over the next craggy bit to get a better view. But up there we could see an even nicer spot a few hundred feet above, so we scrambled up it. In no time at all we were standing on a huge patch of snow at the summit of a mountain only a few feet short of a Munro. There were some hill-walkers with ice-axes coming towards us from the other side of the hill, and I was trying to look as though I meant to come hill-walking dressed like a hairdresser's receptionist. Oh the disgrace and dishonour, not to mention the danger and stupidity.

Another piece of divine retribution for all those hours spent ticking others off came relatively recently. I interviewed Donald Watt, the leader of the Lochaber Mountain Rescue Team, and one of the things we talked about, both nodding sagely in agreement, was that people sometimes wear very stupid things on the hill. We swapped a few anecdotes about buffoons we had encountered and then went our separate ways, hands thrust deep into our respective double-thickness, Gortex, all-weather, storm-force shell outers. A few weeks later I met him in a wild part of Laggan. He was in his climbing gear, had an ice-axe, crampons, and a double-thick Gortex, all-weather, storm force shell outer. I was wearing a nylon fun-fur leopardskin coat, a hat with funny floppy bits for ears, pink fluorescent lipstick, and a pair of short sailing wellingtons. I am not even going to attempt to tell you why I was so attired, or guess at why fate should have made Donald and his equally well-equipped companions with me. Men tend to be up ahead, gaining a rise, stopping suddenly and hissing 'Shooosh! Over there! Look!' By the time we arrive on tip-toe to the spot, whatever it was has either gone or revealed itself to be a log. At least with newt searching you can pick one up and share it round if you find one.

Birds of prey cause a lot of argument on a walk. Not admittedly as much as the argument about whether you can see Schiehallion or not, but certainly enough to end in tears. It is extremely difficult to spot a species from below. Books tell you how, with diagrams and illustrations explaining wing span and feather patterns, but everybody always gets it wrong. The most common exclamation is 'Och, it's only a crow'. I'm not sure how crows feel about this. If I were a member of a species, highly evolved and perfectly adapted to a life among craggy rocks, pecking out the odd lamb's eye, devouring a few mice, picking through a nice gamey carcass occasionally, but mostly just hovering gracefully around on thermals below cliffs, I would take great exception to being described as 'just' a crow. But there is a real class system in spotting wildlife. Crows may do much the same sort of thing as buzzards and eagles but, since there are so many of them, the luckless crows are ignored. An eagle is greeted by sharp intakes of breath from those who spot them, as they reach for their binoculars and cameras. Crows, like the ones that hover round the summit of Buchaille Etive Mor, could fly in a pyramid formation and play the trumpet and walkers would still look the other way.

Deer ruin their chances of being awesome beasts, providing a rare and special experience to those who spot them, by standing in massive herds all along the verge of the A9 looking glum, and grouse lose points for frightening you half to death by crashing out of the heather from under your feet screeching like banshees. This can be multiplied manyfold in its unpleasantness, if you are a woman emptying your bladder at the time. However, I adore the chance to see wildlife in Scotland and am only too acutely aware of how fragile its future is. I have been lucky enough to stroke porpoises from a rowing boat in Loch Torridon, swim in a deep burn with a baby otter in Ardnamurchan and help clear somebody's cottage loft out of a deep pile of pine marten droppings. OK, the last one wasn't so lucky.

The more you walk, especially alone, the more chance you have of wildlife encounters, and you will hopefully realize what a precious pocket of wilderness the Scottish Highlands provide. What a sad creature I'd be if I couldn't promise future children black, peaty lochans full of newts, hillsides teeming with deer, hares and stoats and skies full of soaring majestic birds. No matter what the future holds for the next generation and the delicate trembling wilderness, at least we can promise our children and grandchildren one sure thing. There will be no polecat with young at post number seven on the nature trail.

 Fort William, Loch Linnhe and Loch Eil from Carn Mor Dearg

Looking south towards Loch Quoich

▶ Looking east along Loch Laggan

◀ Above the clouds on the Cairn Liath ridge en route to Creag Meagaidh

▲ Beinn Alligin

▶ Looking towards Kishorn from Ben Damph

Looking west to Loch Morar from Sgurr Thuilm

▲ Looking north along the Devil's Ridge towards Sgurr a' Mhaim

▲ Looking out to the Inner Hebrides

▲ Sgurr Alasdair and the Great Stone Shoot

▶ A scrambler out of her depth

Beinn Eibhinn To Carn Dearg

Beinn Eibhinn; 1100m; (OS Sheets 41 and 42; 449733); M47.
Aonach Beag; 1114m; (OS Sheets 41 and 42; 458742); M38.
Geal-Charn; 1132m; (OS Sheet 42; 471745); M25.
Carn Dearg; 1034m; (OS Sheet 42; 504764); M95.

THERE'S SOMETHING PARTICULARLY DELICIOUS about mountains that are hidden away far out of sight from any road, and Carn Dearg, near Loch Pattack, is a prime example. Although its giant neighbour, Ben Alder, can be viewed from the A9 at the top of Loch Ericht, and the peak further west along its ridge, Aonach Beag, can be seen briefly from the A86 if you're not fishing about for an extra strong mint in the glove compartment, Carn Dearg reveals itself only to those prepared to sweat a bit.

I'd lusted after these peaks for some time, but a decision has to be made about how to get at them. To start from Dalwhinnie means a huge walk along the northern shore of Loch Ericht, and possibly an overnight stop at Culra

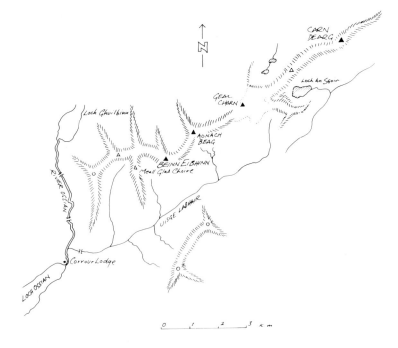

bothy at the base of Carn Dearg, not a pleasant thought when you remember that bothies are always full of smelly men, in even smellier sleeping-bags. Of course this is where a mountain bike could come in handy, but you'd have to put up with walkers pointing at you and shouting 'tosser', and landowners chasing after you with a stick as another slice of expensive path slides into the burn after being cut neatly away by fat tyres.

Then there is the Corrour option. A train will take you to Corrour halt, where a Youth Hostel can be found, leaving you with miles to walk up Loch Ossian before you can even see the ridge.

Finally you can walk in from the A86, an eight- or nine-mile hike, and then start the climb. Not looking good so far, you might think, but then I'm a lucky lass. I've been friends for a few years with the head stalker of Corrour estate, Ted Piggott, and his wife Theresia. That means not only do I get a glass of beer and a scone by the fire, and the chance to pat one of their huge pack of gorgeous shiny dogs, but if I ask politely and don't step on the Jack Russell, I also get permission to bring my car along the private road. Not much help to you, I know, but why should I fib and say I walked in?

It's pretty good knowing someone who lives and works on a big Highland estate if you want to sort out your attitude to the big debate on stalking and access. Ted and I will never see eye to eye about his clients, whom he likes, respects and positively enjoys dragging over hills to bag stags, whereas I loathe these numbskulls who think killing is 'sport'.

Ted's killing is of quite a different nature. Far from

being sport, it's his job to keep herds in check and make sure these 'sportsmen' don't leave an animal wounded and in pain from their hopeless attempts to shoot it, and his respect for living things is acute. He'll do daft things, like making all the stag ponies step aside on the path to avoid treading on a slug. This gives me the terrible dichotomy of knowing that during the stalking season I would dearly love to ruin the day for the fat boors crawling all over Scotland, puffing in their tweeds, but I would hate to disturb Ted and his colleagues at their job, which pays their grocery bills and is their only source of income. So I respect the access restrictions for the sake of Ted and those like him, but I reserve the right in the pub to stick out my tongue and make rasping noises at those men with wallets instead of penises, who think that pulling the trigger and gleefully watching a beautiful stag's legs buckling beneath it as it dies is somehow a sign of manliness.

Of course you don't have to keep off land during the stalking season if you don't want to, since trespass in Scotland is contained within the civil and not the criminal law. That means that it's practically impossible for a landowner to enforce restrictions unless you're setting fire to his house or driving a JCB over his grouse moor. But let's not be stupid about the freedom we enjoy. If you knew Ted, and you probably do judging by the amount of Christmas cards he gets, then you would think twice about being wicked and disruptive for the sake of it. There are plenty of mountains with no stalking to keep you busy during autumn.

Of course sometimes landowners get wildly out of hand

and need a bit of a spanking (other than the one that some already pay for in their strange London clubs). For instance there is one chap in the Kintail area who tries to keep the Mountain Rescue team off his land, not just during their exercises but also in times of actual rescue. Behaving like that, he can hardly be surprised if walkers are tempted to march on to his land in the height of the season playing the bagpipes and accompanied by a 70-strong male voice choir. The sad thing is such behaviour will only end up getting the poor stalker or ghillie the sack so it's not worth the trouble. If a 'keep out' sign annoys you, stop and think of the stalker and his family before you do anything silly, and even if the whole issue of land use and access in Scotland enrages you, remember the place for a protest is not on the hill, but in the ballot box.

Anyway, being in the fortunate position to be able to drive along the road to Corrour, although my car suspension didn't agree it was so fortunate, a companion and I set off for the first peak, Beinn Eibhinn from halfway along the road, above the river Ghuilbinn. We were in a perfect position to attack the mountain from its north side once we had dropped down and crossed the river. For most of the year the river is deep, wide and impossible to cross without stripping off, but the ordnance survey map showed a bridge exactly in our path. Don't always rely on the bridges marked triumphantly on your map. This structure was only the remains of a bridge, and necessitated a crossing hanging on to one piece of rusty wire while balancing on another single line swinging perilously below. Of course you really

shouldn't use such a dangerous structure, and if Ted
Piggott spotted you at it he'd doubtless give you a
row. But the alternative of taking our clothes off on
this nippy morning, and wading across a fast-flowing,
icy river with our clothes on our heads, was not an
attractive one. So we swung across like two trapeze artists
failing an audition for Billy Smart's circus, and headed
gratefully up the glen towards the ridge.

It's a long, slow trudge up to Beinn Eibhinn, but with
the pleasure of experiencing a sense of space quite unlike
anywhere else. This is wild, open country with sweeping
views across forests and rivers to the peaks of Creag
Meagaidh and Beinn a' Chaorainn in the north, and the
hills that surround Corrour and Loch Ossian to the west
and south. Loch Ghuilbinn is particularly beautiful and,
as we climbed, a herd of deer miles below ran splashing
across the neck of the loch, throwing up fountains of
water that sparkled in the sunlight.

If Ted is reading this, they didn't see or smell us,
honest!

On attaining the summit, it's a bit of a shock to
see how far down the ridge drops round the lip of
the corrie before climbing back up to Aonach Beag,
but it snakes invitingly away to the east, presenting an
irresistible walkway into untamed terrain.

It has to be said that this is a massive walk, particularly for you if you don't know Ted, and you could
certainly fill a day with only these two peaks. However,
once up there the temptation to carry on is too strong,
so choose a day early in the summer if you have no
will-power to stave off the seduction of the tops. At

Looking south towards the ridge from Creag Meagaidh

least you'll have enough light to return, even if you've worn your legs down to a stump.

From the crest of Aonach Beag is a rare and spectacular view of Ben Alder. This is a hugely complex hill that's seen many a Munroist stand vacantly at Dalwhinnie trying to puzzle out what the hell is going on up there. From this vantage point it becomes clearer, showing its rounded back to the west and a steep series of crags, cliffs and gullies to the north and east. An even better view of it is a later reward at the summit of Carn Dearg, when you can clearly see the sharp high gully that slices Ben Alder in two, with a remarkably large high-level loch nestling between the summit and the top of Beinn Bheoil. Ben Alder has always seemed as impenetrable to me as a hi-fi magazine, but from up on the ridge it gives away its secrets and reveals a relatively simple ascent from the west up a long, inclining slope.

There's an astoundingly dark deep gorge dividing Ben Alder and Aonach Beag called the Bealach Dubh, through which runs an eerie stalkers' path. If there hasn't been an historic massacre there, then somebody ought to organize one, or at least a bit of a tiff, to do justice to its shadowy, sombre sentinels of cliffs. Perhaps someone could lure some 'sportsmen' in tweeds into its tenebrous depths, where we could leap down on them from a great height to tweak their noses and fill their plus fours with cornflakes. That would do the trick.

Although we were walking on a sunny, but chilly, Saturday in early June, the ridge was completely deserted, a great bonus considering the weekend traffic on most Munros. But as we continued on to the broad plateau of

Geal-Charn, not named on the ordnance survey map, we saw a figure in the distance. I have already mentioned my contempt for those who don't say hello on hills, so as this soul was alone I prepared to greet him or her heartily. The tricky thing is to judge at what point to raise a hand in salutation. Too soon and both parties are left grinning at each other soundlessly for a quarter of a mile, unsure as to what happens next. Too late and the greeting is grunted as an afterthought as you both pass only feet away from each other.

This walker solved the problem. He altered his course to avoid us altogether. Finding myself mildly offended, and not to be denied contact, I shouted and waved from at least half a mile away. A hand was raised limply although he didn't appear to look up. A thin line, I think, between a man in total harmony with peace and solitude and a grumpy, unsociable, old sourpuss.

It's at the top of Geal-Charn that you must make the decision to go back or carry on to Carn Dearg. The problem is that while the previous three Munros are all close together, Geal-Charn is bloody miles away. We decided that although we were tired we might never be given another chance to get at it so easily. Ted might decide he doesn't like me any more, that I laugh too loudly or drink too much of his beer, and then we'd have to get a tent. So we set off down the steep easterly flank of the mountain, alongside a spectacular waterfall that incredibly was still partially frozen in June. It drops into Lochan an Sgoir over steep cliffs and a path of sorts zig zags its way in tandem, until you reach a rounded ridge between two scrumptious corries.

This is a magical place, and fatigue is suppressed by wonder, especially if you had a pork pie before the descent.

A long pull up to the summit, Carn Dearg pays a dividend of an uninterrupted view north and east, to Loch Pattack, the snaking gash of Loch Ericht and, as I mentioned, south to offer a clear perception of the hanging valley of Ben Alder.

Below nestles the Culra Bothy, surrounded by a thick green fog emanating from its occupants' underpants, and to the north-west is the astonishing side of Beinn a' Chlachair. Astonishing to me at least, since it's a mountain I'm intimate with from its friendly north face, and had little notion of its dramatic cliffs lurking sneakily behind me all those times I sat innocently chewing chocolate at the top.

Instead of retracing our steps, we dropped down into An Lairig, the glen between the ridge and the deceitful Beinn a' Chlachair, mainly because Mr OS map assured us with a neat dotted line that there was a stalkers' path there. Forget it. It barely exists, and gives up completely after Dubh Lochan, leaving the hoodwinked walker to stumble back through huge peat hags, and over miles of outrageously rough ground.

Crossing the shoogly bridge back to the road, we looked like two carcasses hanging from an abattoir refrigerator hook. I've seen more energy in a darts champion. We were exhausted.

Since we could barely stand up or speak there was little point in dropping in on Ted and Theresia, although perhaps they wouldn't have noticed much difference in my case, given as they are to ply me with drink. But the day was a stunner, with only one sighting of a human being in 13 miles of walking. It was only later that I came up with a theory for his reticence to stop and speak. Because we had the car, something other walkers couldn't do, we were approaching Carn Dearg just after lunch. This would have been impossible unless we camped at the foot of Beinn Eibhinn, or had started from Loch Ossian at dawn, or were two gold medallist fell-runners. Maybe he was cheesed off meeting people so far along the ridge without explanation as to their start point. My companion had a more plausible theory. He said I waved at the poor man like a loony.

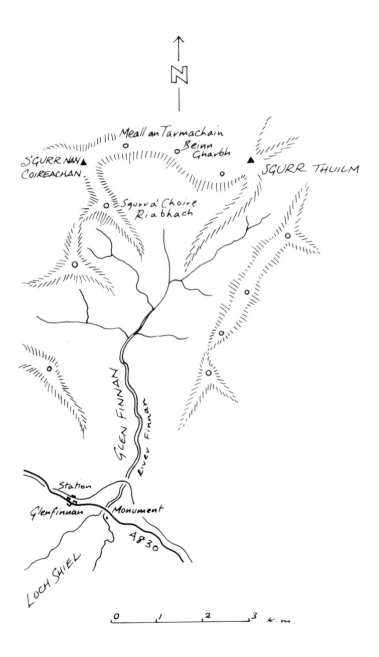

Sgurr Nan Coireachan to Sgurr Thuilm

Sgurr nan Coireachan; 956m; (OS Sheet 40; 903880); M202.
Sgurr Thuilm; 963m; (OS Sheet 40; 939879); M189.

THOSE WHO LEAVE THE WEST HIGHLAND LINE AT
Fort William are missing possibly the most beautiful
section of railway in Europe, that is the line that runs
westward to Mallaig. Ha! I can hear critics cry. How
can I award it such heady status when there are railway
links snaking between the mighty Alps that make the
West Highland line look like Clapham junction? The
fact is that nowhere on earth sketches such a dramatic
and romantically loaded countenance like the north-west
of Scotland, and believe me, I've poked around the world
a bit. Heavy precipitation sets it aside from its bone-dry
Alpine and Himalayan rivals, lavishing a verdure on
Scotland, and a primeval quality to its light that is
quite unique. And where else on earth would a through
train from Glasgow to Mallaig unhitch the guard's van at

Fort William that contained your bike, without breaking the news to you until Lochailort?

My jaw was on the carriage floor the first time I took the train to Mallaig. Even though my bike and rucksack were miles away on the platform of Fort William station, I cannot remember being so profoundly moved on public transport, unless you count the time I thought I saw Sean Connery on the Piccadilly Line.

One of the many highlights is the view down Loch Shiel from Glenfinnan, a vista that has been reproduced many times on gaudy retouched 60s' postcards, and on calendars handed out at Christmas by firms who manufacture ball-bearings. The landscape is rugged and savage, despite a preponderance of caravans, aluminium chairs and fat people with flasks cluttering up the winding road that runs parallel to the railway for the majority of the journey. Readers hardly need me to remind them that the simple but magnificent monument at the head of Loch Shiel is to commemorate the 1745 Jacobite rebellion against English domination. English tourists might like to be reminded that the ghastly visitor centres, the scant toilet facilities and the gruesome catering in the West Highlands of Scotland are there to get you back for the fact you won.

I fell madly in love with this area of Scotland the first time I set eyes on it, and subsequently crawled all over it for years, marvelling at how many caves Bonnie Prince Charlie managed to occupy in his escape from the Redcoats. Old Charlie must have had a bit of a penchant for potholing judging by the amount of time he spent in every rock crevice north of Carlisle, but I prefer to suspend my scepticism and believe that the great man did indeed peel off his powdered wig and roll out a sleeping-bag in all the places that maps and local handouts would have us believe.

I can picture the romantic scene now. Prince Charlie's servants ushering him urgently on to a boat, looking anxiously over their shoulders to check that no traitor has deceived them and given away the location of the Prince's departure, when suddenly the Prince spies a dark hole some miles away on the side of a hill.

'Attendez!' he will say. 'Voilà! Un autre cave.'

The luckless servants trudge resignedly towards the recess. By this time, the Prince's obsession with caves has grown to such a fever pitch that his servants are barely given time to unpack his toothbrush before he spies another gash in the rock, this time many countless miles away.

'Voilà! Un autre cave là-bas!'

Perhaps it's just as well we lost the battle. If you believe all the tourist literature, Charlie, had he come to power, would have made it compulsory to live in rock fissures. Still, a better solution than Mrs Thatcher's legacy, where a mock Georgian red brick house on a speculative builder's estate, with bottle glass windows and a mock doric columned portico is considered desirable. Give me Charlie's cave any day.

Given the rugged nature of the area, I was shocked, indeed horrified, to find that although it contained several hundred of Prince Charlie's caves, it only boasted three Munros. How could Mother Nature have dealt such a savage blow? It's claimed, perhaps unsurprisingly, that the Young Pretender also spent a night out on one

of the three, Sgurr Thuilm. Mind you, if the tourist board
thought they could get away with it, they'd probably
claim he spent an afternoon at the local petrol station,
buying some anti-smear windscreen wash and a fan belt,
before moving on to a gift shop to purchase a handmade
stuffed velvet Loch Ness monster and having an appreci-
ative sniff at the perfumed candle display.

When such a large area reveals it has very few tall peaks
then you can bet your last Mars Bar they'll be stunners.
As a birthday celebration some time ago, I set off with
a companion to conquer the two more accessible ones,
Sgurr Thuilm and Sgurr nan Coireachan.

The starting point is very conveniently from the visitor
centre's car park in Glenfinnan. A malinger round the
monument is worth your while, if only for the extraordinary view down Loch Shiel and to reassure yourself that
you will soon be leaving behind all the people milling
idly around their coaches, to whom 1745 means quarter
to six.

The first part of the walk kicks off up a private road
gliding beneath a fabulous railway viaduct, the very one
from which I had gazed in my bike-less train down the
length of Loch Shiel for the first time some ten years
earlier. There is a package holiday that runs steam trains
up and down the line during the summer, carrying rich
tourists dressed in dinner-jackets and gowns, who scowl
sternly from their carriage windows when the train is
stranded at obscure little Scottish stations. Dozens of
people with rucksacks glare back at them from the platform as they wait for their substandard 'Sprinter' to turn
up; wet, cold and miserable perhaps, but at least secure

in the knowledge that they will eventually travel through the same scenery without parting with their life savings. As we passed under the viaduct that day, one of these steam trains passed overhead, in a cloud of champagne and Chanel fumes. Some find this special reproduction steam train moving and nostalgic. I find it to be an irritating reminder that the solid rail service taken for granted by this part of the country, the one that provides an essential lifeline spring, summer, autumn and winter, is eventually going to be lost to these seasonal theme-park trucks full of florid, truffle-guzzling lounge lizards.

Judging by the amount of Kodak film expended by watching tourists in the seconds it took the train to cross the viaduct, I was alone in my seething contempt for the caviar wagon. It's a pretty sight all right, even if sparks do set fire to the dry grass on either side of the track, enraging landowners. But a prettier sight would be more frequent diesel trains packed with local people returning from shopping trips and visits to Glasgow and Fort William.

The road is a Land-Rover track, and makes easy going and scenic walking alongside the River Finna until you reach Corryhully Lodge. The Scottish Mountaineering Club's Munros book very politely describes this building as 'extraordinarily out of character with its surroundings'. As understatements go, it's a beauty – a bit like saying the *Sun* newspaper is not quite as good as *The Independent*. Why a laird would build such a strange, suburban, concrete monstrosity in a remote and beautiful glen is open to debate. Perhaps an agricultural supplier was giving them away free with every 200 gallons of sheep dip. Just ignore it if you can, and follow the river up the glen until you see and understand the nature of the impressive Coire Thollaidh. From here you can choose either peak as your first, complete the ridge and return to the same point at the river, but it's recommended that you traverse east to west taking in Sgurr Thuilm as Munro number one.

It's not a hard walk up the spur that leads to the summit, and the lust to be able to see far into the rough bounds of Knoydart hiding behind Sgurr Thuilm will motivate even the most indolent hiker. The view is astonishing. The northern slopes of Sgurr Thuilm sweep down to Glen Dessarry, a favourite Knoydart walk-in route from lovely Loch Arkaig. And indeed, from this lofty site Loch Arkaig itself is a vision to make you burst into song.

I'm not sure why Knoydart has 'rough bounds', any more than any other wild area. It may be remote and staggeringly beautiful, but there's no need to show off. Letterewe forest doesn't exactly have 'smooth edges', nor does Rannoch Moor have 'tame perimeters'. So what if Knoydart's bounds are a bit rough? I suspect somebody invented the macho tag to keep out people who buy stripey picnic wind-breaks from the Argos catalogue.

'Ooh, I don't think we should go in there, dear. They say it has very rough bounds.'

Whatever the reason, its landscape fascinates, with unrelenting ripples of rugged hills and deeply pitted glens rising to a clutch of mighty Munros. Knoydart is a delight, looking mouth-watering from the Glenfinnan tops, and you can keep gazing at it longingly as you walk west from Sgurr Thuilm, round the rim of its heroic corrie towards Sgurr nan Coireachan. The treat here is a view that encompasses a glimpse of Loch Morar, that deep narrow gash of water that snakes from the foothills of Sgurr nan Coireachan to the loch's name-sake settlement of Morar on the coast below Mallaig. It's only the eastern end of Loch Morar that deserves a visit for aesthetes, since the coastal end is, like all the lovely settlements on this divine coast, completely ruined by ugly estates of hideous bungalows and cara-van sites that turn the stomach. Greater peace could be found on a boating pond in Regent's Park than at the populated end of poor Loch Morar in summer, with speed boats raping its once enigmatic waters and queues of cars waiting for senior citizens in their caravans to unblock the single track road where they have parked in a passing place to brew up a cuppa. But from the peace of your Munro, all such regrets at its passing as a place of tranquillity vanish and it unveils its wil-der delights at the east to those who come by foot and not by knob-head's speed boat.

What a place to spend a birthday. I was elated by the two peaks, but forgetful of how long the walk out would be. The descent from the second Munro was knee-wrenching, and although it's a relief to regain the track in the glen, it's not such a relief to remember how far away the starting point is.

Ugly as Corryhully Lodge is, you wouldn't say no to be-ing asked in for a cold beer as you passed, as long as no-one you knew saw you go in. I'll wager the Young Pretender was invited in for a Grolsch on his way back from a cave.

My beer was to be in a posh hotel where I was being treated for my birthday, and after the heaven of getting out of a T-shirt that was generating its own new species of life in the arm pits, and into a hot bath, I looked forward to discussing the day eagerly with my companion. I was asleep after the crême brulée.

A Roof Over Your Head

MUNROS. THEY'RE ALL OVER THE PLACE. THAT means that no matter where you live, you're going to stop overnight from time to time. If you have already rejected hotels as too pricey, and youth hostels as too lugubrious, then two further types of accommodation spring to mind when we consider the problem of finding accommodation in the wild and lonely Scottish hills: bothies and tents.

I have nothing against tents. I spent most of my childhood holidays chasing our tent along the tops of cliffs in the middle of the night as gale-force winds carried it towards the sea. Of course we had a rather unsuitable contraption, described as a 'continental' tent. That means it was for use in climates and countries so benign that the natives require no shelter at all, and where a tent is more or less a decorative affectation. Pitched on the machair in Sutherland, however, it proved to be as useful as holding a tea towel over your head. The concept of these 'continental' Wendy Houses with little canvas

An innocent bothy conceals stinking climbers

porches, plastic see-through windows and PVC checked
curtains could only have been dreamed up by someone
who has never been two degrees north of the equator.
Still, it provided the Gray family with regular exercise,
so often did we pursue it over large tracts of Scotland
as the tent tried to escape home to warmer climes in
the south, flapping its PVC accessories like the wings of
a large, wounded goose trying to take off.

Serious walkers and climbers, however, have no such
problems in their neat storm-force tents. These little
units boast they can withstand even the fiercest tempest,
allowing the owner to remain snug and comfortable inside
as the elements rage outside. At least that's what the
catalogue says. My idea of being snug and comfortable is
sitting in an armchair by a log fire, with a pair of slippers
on and someone to bring me soup. A damp sleeping-bag
on a lumpy ground sheet, under canvas that drips and
flaps like the sails of a round-the-world yacht, falls pretty
short of the mark. Yet camping is often the only way to
get near the mountain of your choice, especially when
you choose to ascent some of the more remote peaks.
Since this is the case, it's important to make the best
of it and follow some basic rules that will aid you to
master the art of castrametation.

Travel light. This means sacrificing the crate of export
and the three pounds of reheatable madras curry in a
Tupperware box, and replacing them with objects for your
more immediate use, like the tent. The spartan nature
of camping requires that you live on dehydrated food,
and since at the time of going to print no manufacturer
has come up with dehydrated beer, enforced sobriety will

be a big feature of your expedition. This perhaps, is a blessing in disguise. Emerging from a tent at 6.30 in the morning, desperate for the toilet, but too cold and stiff to move from your reeking sleeping-bag, the last thing you need to deal with is a hangover. Mind you, a hangover is pretty similar to the way you'll feel anyway, so you won't notice the difference.

If you're camping in the wilderness on your own, don't let imagination get the better of you. It's remarkable how similar an owl hooting can sound to a homicidal, horny-clawed, hairy, fanged demon from the bowels of Hell about to rip through the canvas and tear your throat out with a gurgling, raspy cackle. Easy mistake. A good tip to avoid the terrors of the night is simply to imagine where you are in the daylight, and by picturing the pleasant surroundings of your tent in brilliant sunshine, the dark night will hold no satanic secrets. This tip does not apply if you are camping at Aviemore however, where imagining your surroundings in daylight is worse than anything Hell can come up with.

You must take a pair of fine-denier stockings with you. This is not so you can cross-dress in the privacy of wild open country, or perform a stick-up on a youth hostel and rob them of the night's takings of £14.95, but to put over your head when the midges come out. There are no words to describe the profound horror of these beasts, but 'aaaaaargh!' will do for now. The perfect weather for camping – a still, warm night with a gigantic pastel-coloured moon reflecting dreamily in a glassy loch – is coincidentally the perfect night for the midges to chew your ass off. Grown men buckle under the fear that

these relentless, dancing grey clouds bring. Men who can
cling to overhanging rocks thousands of feet above their
companions, men who climb into perilous situations in
the knowledge they are inches from death, men who are
strong enough and man enough to meet any physical
challenge, these are the men who call for their mum when
they find they left the Jungle Formula back in the car.

Your canvas shelter has no defence against the midge,
and the only course of action is to spray the inside of
the tent with the strongest insect repellent on the market, preferably something banned in all other European
countries, and then dive into the sleeping-bag and cover
your head, trying hard not to inhale the toxic gases.
Of course you will wake up in the morning with a
nervous disorder and a slightly lower IQ, but at least
you won't have any itchy red lumps.

The only other piece of important advice is that,
although you can walk anywhere in Scotland, you are not
entitled to camp without permission. I suppose this is sensible. After all a walker is probably unlikely to take an axe
to some prime woodland, build a fire, get a guitar out and
sing *Kumbaya my Lord* all night. The law therefore is there
to protect the landowner. Not because of his trees, you
understand, but because no-one can be expected to put up
with someone singing *Kumbaya*. So choose your site carefully. If you knock at the door of the gamekeeper's house
and he comes to the door wearing an antler head-dress, a
black satin robe with a pentangle on it, and is holding a
headless bleeding chicken in one hand, then even if he
gives you permission to camp, think about going to a B &
B. Some country folk are best left to their own devices.

A bothy is supposed to be easier. For those who have never had the experience, a bothy is a hut, either a renovated ruin or a specially built shack in the heart of the wilderness that walkers can use if they need shelter. The drawback is that lots of people use them and that lots and lots of people will want to use it on precisely the night you require to be there. Nothing wrong with that, you may say. A bit of companionship with fellow climbers and walkers is just the job at the end of a hard day. A sing-song round the fire perchance, a few spooky tales to swap, and then a friendly round of goodnights before slipping off to dreamland on a clean and functional bunk. Nice theory. Try coping with a party of underprivileged schoolchildren from a housing estate in Manchester with a near-hysterical social worker, a ghetto blaster and some crisp bags to sniff glue, two glum shaven-headed squaddies with flatulence, and a computer programmer from Maidstone who wants to tell you about why his promotion fell through, and then with one eye twitching, accuses you of having stolen his processed cheese.

Used properly, bothies are places of great convenience and delight, but do remember a couple of important points. Don't assume you will find shelter in a bothy and walk into the wilderness without an alternative. Sometimes bothies are locked, particularly during the stalking season, and very often you open the door to find there are 75 people crammed into a shack built to accommodate 15. If you do manage to find a place in one, you must tidy it up when you're ready to leave and remember to take your litter with you. People treat this last request in a very strange way. They take almost everything home with them except whisky bottles. These bottles are left with a candle rammed into the neck and therefore presumably considered useful. However, when the summer is over and the bothy is left with 200 whisky bottles, each sporting a candle stump in the neck, their usefulness has to be questioned. Why do people think that inserting a candle into something they have no further use for renders it an indispensable household utensil instead of litter they should be taking home in their rucksacks? Perhaps to avoid taking anything home from the bothy at all, you could stick a candle in some old bacon fat, or a UHT milk carton. How about a candle on a piece of toast or in half a grapefruit? Of course to avoid digging latrines, you could also stick a candle in whatever drips out of your bottom. That should at least get the point over to the whisky bottle interior designers.

Don't expect to have sex in a bothy either. If you've just done a 12-mile ridge-walk then I'm sure nothing will be further from your thoughts, but if you plan a weekend away with a person you've fancied for ages and somehow end up heading for a bothy, unless you are totally alone any thought of a fumble in the sleeping-bag should be out of the question. There is nothing more anti-social than other people at it when you are trying to get some kip. It's also rather annoying if you're on your own, a bit like watching someone eating a three-course meal when you have some dry toast and a pickled onion. So stick to your own tent if you want a snog.

As a final word, for those who are novices in the world of finding somewhere to sleep in the wilds, I can be of some assistance. I have a 'continental' tent for sale, complete with stylish porch, PVC window and curtains. Simply send me a large cheque and I will provide you with the ordnance survey co-ordinates of its last sighting.

An Gearanach To Sgurr A' Mhaim

An Gearanach; 982m; (OS Sheet 41; 188670); M162.
Stob Coire a' Chairn; 981m; (OS Sheet 41; 185661); M165.
Am Bodach; 1032m; (OS Sheet 41; 176651); M96.
Sgor an Iubhair; 1001m; (OS Sheet 41; 165655); M49.
Sgurr a' Mhaim; 1099m; (OS Sheet 41; 165667); M133.

PLANNING AN EXPEDITION OF SEVERAL MUNROS is an exciting business. In fact planning any route that you've made up yourself across wild land is fun, unless you're doing so to escape from someone who is trying to kill you or lock you up.

Mind you, Richard Hannay in John Buchan's *The Thirty-Nine Steps* planned his route because people were trying both to kill him and lock him up, and he still seemed to have some fun. But then right-wing, upper-class fictional characters would have fun even if tentacled Martians were chasing them through sewage. There's always a girl of good breeding to marry and a wise old

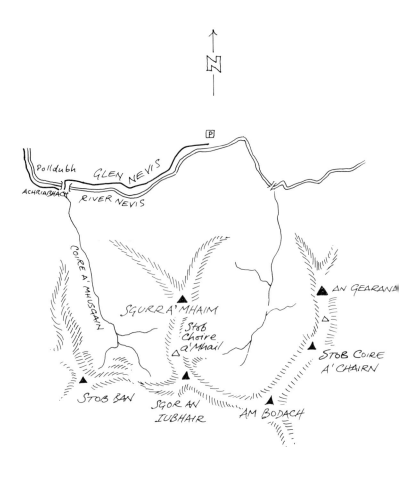

servant to welcome them home and run them a bath on page 342.

But since none of that applies to you, you will know what I mean and probably share my fondness for Munro window-shopping. Mine takes place in my flat, all over the living-room carpet, with maps spread out like prayer mats and cats lying triumphantly and with great precision on the co-ordinates that are of particular interest.

Such is the entertainment value of working out your own routes that I remain baffled by those who think the West Highland Way is a good idea. There are lots of ways to walk to Fort William if that's what you fancy, except now one of them is littered with lots of wooden posts with painted thistles, and hundreds of people trudging about who never thought of walking to Fort William until someone gave them the West Highland Way guide book for their Christmas. Live and let live I say, but unless I want to be certain of constantly bumping into parties of rambling Rotarians, I think I will keep off these organized highways. Some of the larger groups of Munros demand personal route planning, since the permutations of how one may bag them are endless. The Mamores are just such a group of mountains, containing 11 Munros placed magnificently between Loch Leven and Glen Nevis, and since there is easy access from both north and south you have all manner of decisions to take about where to start and finish, how many to do and in what order.

A friend and I spread the maps out, moved the cats, and decided to pick off five Munros that form a horseshoe ridge culminating in Sgurr a' Mhaim, and including something ominously titled the Devil's Ridge. This route begins from Glen Nevis and you can take your car up to the head of the Glen and leave it in a packed car park, if you can find a space between the ice-cream vans and hot-dog vendors. You have the choice of being snooty and tutting at people sitting in their cars, packing their faces with hot dogs, or you can pack your own face with a hot dog before you set out. I recommend the latter.

There is a huge sign here below the Allt Coire Giubh-sachan, a steep, slabby waterfall cascading down to the edge of the car park, that yells, 'WARNING! This is not the path to Ben Nevis.' It goes on at some length to persuade people not to climb up this waterfall and muck about in it. It may not be the path, but of course it is perfectly possible, although steep and hard, to get to the summit of Ben Nevis via this corrie although I can think of no mountaineer who would imagine a gushing, torrential waterfall to be the path, take off their socks and shoes and start trying to wade up it.

'Oh look, John! It's a big, deep, fast flowing river. That must be the path to the top. Glad I brought my waterproof trousers.'

'No, Laura, I think you're mistaken. There's a huge deep loch over there. I vote we walk into it and look for the summit under the water.'

Hardly likely.

So one can only surmise that this rather authoritarian sign is aimed at people whose knuckles scrape the tarmac. I'm not complaining. It's a free country and everyone has the right to be mind-numbingly stupid if they want, and subsequently I suppose it's better if they can avoid killing themselves as a direct result. So if the sign saves lives

I'm all in favour of it. I just don't want to see similar signs appearing up mountains as hill-walking grows more popular. Where would it all end? A sign up on the narrowest section of the Aonach Eagach perhaps, reading, 'WARNING! This is not the way to the ladies room in the Kingshouse Hotel. You are on a mountain.' Or one on top of the Inaccessible Pinnacle on Skye urgently declaring, 'WARNING! This is not the way to the ladies room in the Kingshouse Hotel either, in fact this is an even worse mountain and it's on Skye, you imbecile! Glencoe is that way. Mind how you go now, have a nice day!'

Let's leave the mountains wild and dangerous and just make sure we know what we're going to face when we tackle them, and go fully prepared. The whole point is adventure and calculated risk taking. If signs start going up we'll have wrought-iron railings and flowerpots round the trip points next.

A track runs east from the car park, alongside the magnificent Water of Nevis, starting off benignly enough to lure bored coiffured teenagers in high heels along it until they come a cropper as it climbs through the woods and becomes rocky. The river is impressive, tumbling down through a deep gorge, from which it has cut weird and wonderfully shaped holes in the smooth rock. These sparkling crystal green pools look ideal for swimming, but beware dangerous undercurrents, the fact that they are deeper than they look, a temperature cold enough to freeze-dry your internal organs, and an audience of 50 tourists who will stand and watch as you try to get out of the water and back into your underpants with some dignity and without swearing.

Although the path at this stage is packed solid with shuffling picnickers, it's a beautiful little track, especially when it emerges from the gorge and opens up into a wide glen where the Allt Coire A' Mhail tumbles to the Water of Nevis via a narrow and dramatic waterfall. Were you to continue on this path it would take you to Corrour Station on the edge of Rannoch Moor, and judging by the brutal erosion, something exciting and irresistible must be going on up there to lure so many boot-clad walkers along the track. Maybe they're having Acid House parties or car boot sales. All right then, it might just be a fabulous walk, but whatever the reason it's helped wear a deep wide scar up the glen that the scenery could well do without.

But it would be hard to ruin this part of the glen completely. It's almost Himalayan in character, possessing that combination rare in Highland topography, of rugged drama twinned with pastoral tranquillity. It's also alive with midges, which stands in the way of it being a Scottish Shangrila. Hard to picture happy mystical Tibetans dancing mysteriously in their bright robes in a place where two inches of bare skin turns black with the little schmucks in seconds. The only exotic mysterious dance this glen will witness is one where walkers run wildly about in circles waving their arms in alarm, screaming, 'Get them off me!'

There's a bridge across the river consisting of three ropes of thick wire in a V-shape. The crosser is required to tight-rope walk on the single strand below and hold on to the other two other lines for balance. There's no need to use it if the river's not in spate, since you can just as easily hop over some stones in the shallows a few yards

further upstream. But when the snow melts in spring this
crossing is essential, so it's worth trying just for the fun
of it. As we approached, a party of surly children were
being taught how to traverse this wire contraption by an
Outward Bound teacher from the Midlands. The poor
poppets were being forced to attach lifelines to the upper
cables and edge across as though their lives depended on
it. This odd instructor shouted at them constantly in a
tone of voice that suggested they were clinging to a ledge
hundreds of feet above a lava-filled crater, being pursued
by leathery-skinned trolls. In fact they were on a bridge
hanging innocently above two feet of pleasant, placid
water, that on this balmy summer afternoon looked inviting enough to jump into anyway. But this man's job was
the creation of adventure where clearly none was available.

There's definitely money to be made by running an
Outward Bound course. All you have to do is grow a

beard and look rugged, take a bunch of gullible kids
from good homes, make their parents pay through the
nose to let them sleep in bunks and eat beans, and then
pretend that mundane things are difficult or unusual. It
wasn't as if they were heading for the hills. After their
terribly exciting bridge crossing, they hopped back over
the shallows and headed back to their mini-van. I'll bet
he made them rope up to do the dishes.

I think I may start up a course. For only £500 a week
all inclusive, I'll show you how to put on walking boots,
where the zip on your kagoul can be located, how to
prepare a salami sandwich, and what to do if you should
come across a gate. Course members will sleep in a tent
while I take a suite at the Inverlochy Castle Hotel, and
at the end of the week everyone gets an official hand-
written certificate to say they can put on gaiters without
assistance. OK, some courses are good. Don't sue.

When safely across the river, remembering of course
to unclip your lifeline, take off the safety helmet, undo
your life jacket, and slip out of the survival suit, the
route passes beneath the splendid waterfall and starts
to climb up to An Gearanach, not marked by name
on the ordnance survey map. It's a steep ascent but the
compensation is a swift gaining of the ridge. From the
first top there is a breathtaking panorama back across
the glen to the southern slopes of Ben Nevis and Aonach
Beag, but perhaps more thrilling, across the corrie westwards to the goal of Sgurr a' Mhaim.

On a curving ridge-walk like this, the last Munro
staying within sight all the way can either be immensely
heartening or terrifically dispiriting, depending on your

state of exhaustion. At the start, when you still have enough energy to argue if you can see Schiehallion or not, and your first piece of chocolate has yet to be unwrapped, the distant peak beckoning on the far side of the ridge is sensational. After a non-Munro top, An Garbhanach, it's a short pull up to the second peak Stob Coire a' Chairn. Here, the shapely Am Bodach makes you ache to carry on, and although it looks sharp but simple, there is quite a vertigo-inducing section of easy scrambling at the top that may catch those without a head for heights unawares. You will gather I mean it caught me unawares, and in fact it disturbed me that having a bit of a wobbly on something as simple as this did not bode well for the Devil's Ridge, which *The Munros* book described as a section where 'some may welcome the security of a rope'. I blame the fact that a crow chose to hover below me as I scrambled up a tricky bit of path, made more perilous by loose shifting gravel. I wish crows wouldn't do that.

It's on Am Bodach that a lot of people's routes converge. Those who came up from the Kinlochleven side may climb Am Bodach with the plan to turn east and do Na Gruagaichean, or carry on westwards for Stob Ban. Or indeed they could be heading for the two peaks we had just thrashed. So much choice, and so many different ways to traverse this superb maze of peaks and ridges means that there is sometimes a bit of a scrum at these crossroad peaks. It's an amusing game however, as you struggle for a seat out of the wind at the cairn to eat your peanut butter sandwiches, trying to guess which way everyone will go when they smack their lips, wipe their hands on their breeches and get up to leave.

Some may even have come up from the West Highland
Way which runs below Am Bodach in a secluded glen
parallel to Loch Leven. But they're easy to spot. They'll
be searching for a wooden stick with a thistle painted
on it, and discussing the minutes of the last Rotarians'
whist drive subcommittee meeting.

I doubt if our route caused any speculation in others
at all, and so we finished lunch and turned west towards
Sgor an Iubhair. There is a tremendous feeling of comfort
when you finally change direction on such a walk. Since
the final Munro has been with you all the way along, it's
only here that you feel you are now finally making your
way towards it and the conclusion of the walk. But of
course there was still the Devil's Ridge to come. Would
I or would I not welcome the security of a rope? Would I
perhaps welcome the security of a helicopter, or welcome
the security of waking up in bed to find that it was all
a dream and I hadn't actually gone hill-walking at all because I had a date with Gerard Depardieu? Who could
say? There was no sign of this Devil's Ridge and by the
time we reached the summit of Sgor an Iubhair I was
imagining a knife edge of rock, hanging above an abyss
full of red scaly demons, holding pitch forks and hissing
to one another, 'She hasn't got the security of a rope.'

At the summit, however, the ridge reveals all. Rather
disappointingly there is not too much to be scared of in
summer. It's certainly a narrow arête, but I found the
tiny loose stones of Am Bodach's unstable path far more
disquieting than this ridge, with its well-worn, solid path
snaking comfortingly across to the last top between us
and our goal of Sgurr a' Mhaim. However, winter would

transform it into something perilous in the extreme, even with crampons and an axe, and I'd give it a miss during that season unless you're an experienced mountaineer. If anything, by this time I would have welcomed the security not of a rope, but of seeing Sgurr a' Mhaim about a mile closer. It had been a long walk so far, and it wasn't over. The last great pull up the final top was agony. Sgurr a' Mhaim was my 50th Munro, but as I hauled my dejected little body up the last few hundred feet, I was thinking only of rest, not triumph.

But priorities shifted once on the summit. What a place to view not only the entire ridge-walk we had completed, but the majesty of Ben Nevis, the tips of the Glencoe mountains peeking over the edge of the Mamores to the south and the most perfect eagle's eye view up to the head of Glen Nevis. I was an emotional morsel as we headed back.

The minor irritation on returning to the car is that it is directly in front of you as you descend to the north, but there is nowhere to cross the river. You could try of course, but after a colossal, tiring ridge-walk you would be a dingbat even to think of it. So you are forced to swing east again and stumble down through a dense birch forest until you reach the wire bridge, and retrace your steps back along the tourist path.

It was an evening of celebration for me, and after a pint and a half of draught Becks, I would have welcomed the security of a rope.

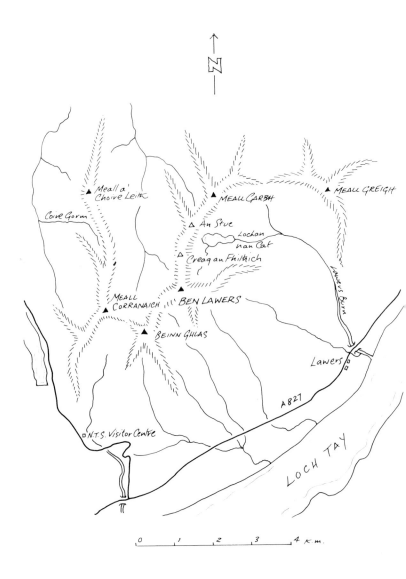

Meall A' Choire Leith To Ben Lawers

Meall a' Choire Leith; 926m; (OS Sheet 51; 612439); M257.
Meall Corranaich; 1069m; (OS Sheet 51; 616410); M65.
Beinn Ghlas; 1103m; (OS Sheet 51; 626404); M45.
Ben Lawers; 1214m; (OS Sheet 51; 636414); M9.

JUST AS I LOATHE THE WORD 'WORKSHOP', I FEEL
queasy when places include the word 'centre'. Shops are
not shops any more, but 'furniture centres', or 'DIY
centres'. The problem is that there is nothing remotely
central about these places at all. More often than not
they are located ten miles outside town under a tin
roof, in wasteland surrounded by a car park the size
of Brazil. Sadly, country folk have caught on. Heritage
Centres compete with Visitor Centres, while Gift Centres
crop up next to Heather Centres. It's only a matter of
time before we will see a Centre Centre, where the
visitor can enjoy a fascinating audio-visual presentation
of the large varieties of Centres throughout Scotland. It

will, of course, be located somewhere so obscure that
Dougie Donnelly will be required to voice-over a map
on a television commercial explaining how you can get
there with the family this Sunday. The only centre I have
time for is the Sea Life Centre near Oban, on account
of a circular tank of herring you can stand under, and
that it has a moray eel. But even it would do itself a
favour if it took the Tippex to its business stationery
and removed that redundant word 'Centre'.

The fact that the ordnance survey map of Ben Lawers
proudly declared a Visitor Centre at the base left me no
choice in the route I was to take to the top. To avoid
it, it meant climbing up from the Glen Lyon side and
attacking the Ben via the three westerly Munros that
share its ridge. Ha! That would show them! No one's
going to make me buy a postcard with a baby otter on
it, or pick up a leaflet on alpine lichens.

So a male companion and I drove up to the starting point in Glen Lyon, a few miles east of Bridge
of Balgie where a bridge crosses the River Lyon to a
cattle farm. The horseshoe ridge that Ben Lawers dominates can be knocked off in a single day if you have
legs of iron, but for a more leisurely exploration of the
hills, Glen Lyon is where to pick off Meall a' Choire
Leith, Meall Garbh, and the more distant Meall Greigh
that turns the horseshoe into an S-shape. All the guide
books insisted that 'fit walkers' could certainly complete the five Munros that loop round from Glen Lyon,
and so vanity compelled us to try.

The beauty and clarity of our spring day was forgotten
momentarily when we lumbered through a mighty ocean

of dung and mud, caused by a recent and substantial visitation from the farmer's cows. Who'd be a cattle farmer? At least sheep trot about doing their own unpleasant things well out of sight of the farmhouse kitchen window, and can be brought home by a couple of mad, slavering collies and a man with a whistle. Cows, on the other hand, saunter around in large malodorous herds, bumping into the Land-Rover, farting and crapping all over themselves and each other, and turn previously walkable paths into evil, bubbling quagmires that leave the unsuspecting trekker caked in cow dung for the remainder of their day. Perhaps that's the reason farmers keep them. A bit of bother with walkers trudging through his land can soon be sorted out by nipping along to an agricultural auction and purchasing some huge stinking cows. The happy landowner can then stand at the window smoking a pipe and wave cheerily at the unwelcome hill-walkers, secure in the knowledge that in a few minutes they will be heading back to the car, steam gently rising from them as they blink in distress from behind grisly face-masks of dung.

I was lucky. The dung only penetrated as far as my upper thigh as we struck up the devastated hillside towards Meall a' Choire Leith. The ascent on to the ridge evolves in easy stages, taking you up over a number of small, craggy knolls until you reach the commodious upper slopes of the Munro. Ben Lawers looks very far away from here, possibly because it is in fact very far away from here, but the walking on this lofty green ridge is so agreeable that the distance still to cover becomes an irrelevance.

On gaining the ridge we walked behind a large group of sprightly, if somewhat sturdy, women well into their 50s,

an unusual and inspiring sight to someone like myself who feels like a wizened wheezing old hag at 32. We discreetly discussed who they might be, and finally placed our bets on either a WRVS ramblers' club from Perth, or a group of senior women's prison officers on an Outward Bound course. As we overtook them, they revealed themselves instead to be German tourists. Perhaps gangs of older women up hills is quite the norm in the Fatherland, and if so it could do with being aped here. It's the old chaps in this country who get to pull on their boots and leave the women behind to a fate of wearing beige coats, having their hair permed and choosing a new tartan plastic cover for the *Radio Times* from the newsagent when they pick up their *People's Friend.* If I can't still clamber up a mountain when I'm 55, subject to health and having both legs of course, I want to be put down humanely.

The rampant sexism of the climbing and walking fraternity over the last 50 years has left a whole generation of older women with the legacy of being expected to have the white-bearded, old sod's tea ready for him on the table when he comes home from a fabulous day out on the hills. She will have spent the last 30 years of their marriage sitting in the passenger seat of the car which she is still unable to drive, disappearing into the kitchen when his climbing friends call round for a beer, and laughing dutifully at his mountain anecdotes over a dinner she has made for his boss. I wish I could give these women their time again, to take them to the hills and show them what they could have shared with their selfish husbands, show them how a ridge-walk compares to a coffee morning in a draughty church hall, and how they could have become more in tune with their spirit and feelings up here than stuck down there watching television soap operas.

At least my generation of women is safe. If you guys think that in our middle age we'll be at a Tupperware party while you do the Skye Ridge, you can roll your tartan shirts up and shove them. Anyway the argument is academic, since by the time I'm 55 the Skye Ridge will be a London-owned Sport And Leisure 'Centre', with most of Glen Brittle bulldozed to provide the car park.

Leaving our Teutonic heroines behind, we carried happily on along the grassy ridge to Meall Corranaich, although a small matter of some concern was that Ben Lawers had started to cloud over. The summit was already in cloud and things weren't improving. It's a long walk to Meall Corranaich and just before the top, the ridge splits away to the west which causes some confusion in poor visibility. At least we reached the summit before the weather slipped across the glen from Ben Lawers to get at us, and we thrilled to the views south and west, with the seductive moss-green hills still sporting small patches of snow.

Because of the closing weather, an element of urgency entered our expedition, and my companion started to speed up his pace so dramatically that within five minutes conversation between us was only possible by semaphore. Not wishing to be a pansy, I stepped up my pace too, but I was no match for the male legs I was pursuing since both of my spindly little limbs could fit into the right leg of his breeches. The drop down from Meall Corranaich and back up to Beinn Ghlas was a great deal more substantial than I would have wished at this point in the walk, keeping in mind that I was hallucinating from the effort of the chase and the subsequent lack of oxygen managing to get anywhere near my lungs via a mouth full of clenched teeth. When I finally caught up with my sprinting friend, who was standing innocently taking a swig from his water bottle, the needles on all my body dials were twitching into red.

We hadn't stopped for lunch yet, but decided that food would be a great incentive to get us up this last steep pull on to the summit of Beinn Ghlas. I was on my knees by the time we unpacked the sandwiches and tried to find the energy to chew, and I recall making small high-pitched squeaking noises in reply to any attempt at a chat. Not only was it getting cold and windy, but it was getting very busy at the top of Beinn Ghlas. People dressed in slacks and trainers kept walking by, saying jolly things to me like, 'Don't worry. Not long 'till the top' and 'It doesn't get any easier, you know!'

Who were these people and what had my state of collapse got to do with them? Anyway, we were at the top already. It was only then I realized that these were the Visitor Centre people on their way to Ben Lawers, pockets stuffed with postcards of eagles and leaflets on natural birch forest regeneration. As soon as I realized they thought I was knackered from the same route they had just walked, I was speechless with indignation. But it's hard to reply to some sweet, well-meaning English family who are making the effort to be sociable, by throwing your tomato at them and yelling, 'What do you know, you lazy bastards? I've already done three Munros.'

I think that may have been construed as impolite, so I smiled and replied that, yes indeed it was still a bit to go before the top, and wow, certainly it was proving mighty tough.

But the day was past its best. Not only was the weather becoming ghastly, with wind and rain starting to turn to gales with snow, the mountain was now full of people walking dogs and putting up umbrellas. We dragged ourselves up the wide, eroded mess of a path that leads to Ben Lawers and up into the storm. I thought the top would never come, but then it's easy to forget this mountain is nearly 4,000 feet.

Someone who couldn't forget that it was nearly, but not quite, that height, was one Malcolm Ferguson who in 1878 became so incensed by Ben Lawers being declared officially under the 4,000-foot mark by means of new surveying techniques, he decided to do something about it. He organized a band of local workers to build a gigantic cairn 20 feet high, thus putting the summit safely above 4,000 feet again. For this promethean task the workers were each paid with a handsome bound volume of Gaelic poetry. Regional councils should take note. When the navvies turn up for their wages on a Friday afternoon after a hard week of digging up roads, try presenting them with a handsome bound volume of Gaelic poetry. Please could I be there when you try it?

Needless to say, the cairn crumbled, probably sabotaged by a disgruntled worker who got home to find he'd already read this particular volume of Gaelic poetry, and Ben Lawers remains at 3,984 feet. For all we knew it could have been 12 feet, since the weather was so bad at the top we could see no further than someone wearing a ski anorak and wellingtons sitting beside us.

We still had one Munro to go in our master plan, which was Meall Garbh to the north of Ben Lawers, but two minutes of huddling behind a rock reminded us that plans can be changed. We abandoned the last Munro, especially as it's a top that can be combined with Meall Greigh to be bagged another day, and staggered down into the long glen that would take us back to our morning starting point.

Once down out of the wind, the weather was bearable again and we could enjoy the intriguing glen pitted with the ruins of ancient shielings either side of the Allt a' Chobhair. There is a profusion of these ruins in this area, a testimony to how heavily and successfully populated it once was. It's eerie walking silently between these ghost summer villages that must have once echoed to children playing, women gossiping and men complaining about being paid for their labours with books of Gaelic poetry. Of course since the shielings were here to provide summer grazing for their cattle, the villages must also have echoed to people splashing about in mud and dung, and laments of, 'Dad, I hate these smelly big things. Why can't we have sheep like the neighbours?'

'Hush, child. They keep the walkers away.'

The whole Loch Tay area has a fascinating and rich history stretching back to prehistoric times, none of which I'm prepared to share with you. Buy a history book.

There is a small dam to pass, and then it's plain sailing all the way back to the car park to live with the shame that we failed to live up to the term 'fit walkers'.

On the way home we stopped off at an alcohol centre and had a pint.

Oh For Pity's Sake, What Now?

SCOTLAND'S MOUNTAINS MEAN SO MANY THINGS
to different people. To the crofters who scraped a
meagre living at their base they were acres of near-
vertical land that couldn't support a turnip. Battling
clans and pursuing Redcoats cursed them for presenting
huge obstacles denying fast military movement around
the Highlands, whereas the Victorians regarded them as
sporting playgrounds and background subject matter for
romantic oil paintings of the fat, unattractive aristocracy
and their useless families. The modern perception of the
hills, however, seems to be that they are one gigantic
Butlin's. Our mountains have survived for millions of
years, bearing witness to a history of violent, volcanic
activity, glaciation and erosion, but ironically it's the
invention of the internal combustion engine and lightweight waterproof clothing that has put them under the
most severe pressure yet. The problem is not necessarily
just the massive increase in numbers of walkers and

climbers, but the fact that people are daily dreaming up new and more ridiculous things to do on the hills for fun.

Of course there has traditionally always been the kind of individual that will view any large feature in the landscape as something to jump off, slide down or swing from on the end of a piece of elastic. They are usually wealthy ex-public school boys, who, since they will never need to work for a living, have little else to occupy them except the pursuit of cheap thrills. Unfortunately, their penchant for the invention of bizarre new ways to tempt the grim reaper has filtered down to us, the lower orders, and we now follow their example.

If climbers hugged themselves in delight in the knowledge that they had the monopoly on daft, death-defying behaviour, their hearts must have sunk to see people above them launch themselves off cliffs, strapped to a parachute. These are paragliders; mad fools who climb to the top of Munros and jump off. Inspiration no doubt came from the Alps, where handsome, tanned young men float around below bright silk parachutes, framed by the sunlit, benign, windless, snow-covered Alps. How the Scottish paragliders imagined this sport would adapt to the arctic, savage, gale-torn mountains of home is anybody's guess, but they appear to be quite happy flapping around in the rain before plummeting out of the sky like Icarus and skidding to an inelegant halt face first in small lochans.

Perhaps my notion of wilderness is romantic and hopelessly out of date, but I have to say that I find paragliding an intrusion. It causes no pollution, either in terms of fuel consumption or noise, yet finding yourself suddenly cowering in the shadow of a huge coloured parachute at the top of a hill where you imagined yourself to be alone, bursts the illusionary balloon of solitude and remote wilderness for me. Perhaps it's because the sport seems ironically so urban that I find it less than thrilling. It belongs somehow with those who hang around speed-boats and water skiers, and who think that Loch Lomond's Duck Bay Marina is 'sporty'.

I'll admit it must be thrilling, but like most thrilling sports the downside is a lot of standing around. You can always tell when people are preparing to partake in a thrilling sport from the small pack of men standing around with their hands in their pockets. This happens on the beach where there is windsurfing, in the car parks and lift stations of ski resorts, when people are hang-gliding or ice-climbing, but most certainly when there is a paraglider about to take off. Perhaps the band of ponderous chaps come with the equipment and can be selected in the shop along with harnesses, clips, body-braces and lightweight aluminium frames.

'Right, sir, that's one parachute, a harness, a safety helmet and a group of five men to watch you with their hands in their pockets. Would you like yuppie windsurfing men, bearded grim-faced mountain men, or the model aeroplane men with flat caps and quilted waistcoats?'

'Well which would you recommend? This'll be my first time.'

'Oh certainly the model aeroplane men. A bit pricey perhaps but they're very good value for money. They'll stand and watch anything for hours.'

So many things can go wrong when you paraglide. Apart from the obvious one which is to jump off the mountain incorrectly and kill yourself, the possibility for public humiliation is delightfully endless. I sat eating my sandwiches in a grumpy sulk at the top of a mountain recently, while the pack of men surrounding a paraglider prepared him for take-off. With a shout and to a chorus of 'Go for it, Kevin!' he ran towards the edge and leapt into the air. Seconds later he was struggling under yards of silk only 20 feet down the other side of the hill, wrestling beneath the parachute like an actor in a soft porn film. Since that was my route home I could glance back every so often and see how the untangling process was going. They took nearly an hour to sort him out.

My only other close encounter with a paraglider was finding one grounded in a quagmire in the Arrochar Alps, where the poor man had come down in the wrong glen, leaving him miles to walk back to any road. To add to his dismay, both his clothing and parachute were so clogged with peat and mud after an interesting landing that I would have paid money to have witnessed, that packing his gear up and walking out with it was out of the question. The luckless creature, who confessed to coming from Leeds as though it were an explanation of the folly, abandoned it all and trudged home like a beaten cur. No doubt his pack of men would have returned later to retrieve it, but it did strike me as a rather unsatisfactory way to spend a day in the hills.

A more significant intrusion into the wilds, certainly in terms of numbers, is the fashion of mountain biking. I've always ridden bikes off the road on to trails to get far into the heart of the country, but they were big, creaky, clanking old things that had to have a puncture repaired

A mountain bike at its most useful – as something to pose on for a photograph

every 20 minutes. So I, foolishly, welcomed the invention of the tough trail bike, designed as it is to handle exactly the kind of unmetalled forest trails and dirt tracks I had previously navigated on something the grocer's boy in a Hovis advert would have ridden.

I began to get nervous when these new fluorescent vehicles started being referred to as 'mountain' bikes. Obviously they couldn't be ridden on a mountain, but magazine articles and newspaper features began treating them as a status symbol, and so every airhead on a salary of over £20,000 a year rushed out to buy one and take it up a mountain. The glowing consumer reports about cycling the peaks and television commercials for aftershave showing hunky men rattling down sheer slopes of scree on bikes made me suspicious. I hired one and went to try it on a mountain. Of course you can't ride it up trackless slopes of heather, peat hags and boulder fields – in fact you have to carry it on your shoulder as soon as you leave any kind of track at all – but it performed brilliantly on the rocky Land-Rover track back down from the hill. I was reassured that the nonsense would stop, and that people would use the bikes merely to get to the base of mountains, where the walk in was prohibitive of completing the hill in a day without some means of transport. I was wrong. A man completed all the Munros with a mountain bike. You'll notice I say 'with' a mountain bike rather than 'on' a mountain bike. I can't imagine he enjoyed much of a free-wheeling, look-no-hands cycle along the Skye Ridge. But why anyone would want to carry a bike up a mountain on their shoulder for the pleasure of being able to bump about on it for tiny, short stretches of flat ridge was completely beyond me. It was their problem, I thought, and they could do what they liked.

Then the invasion started in earnest. Walkers would find themselves diving out of the way on paths, escaping from runaway mountain bikes careering towards them on a mission to deposit their riders in a ditch. Landowners started to complain that the bikes were chewing up their paths, raising the whole ugly debate about access up on to a new plane, and ridge-walks lost some of their grandeur by displaying fat tyre tracks on their grassy sections.

There is one great consolation, however, which is the fact that on a mountain nothing looks stupider than someone on a bike. If paragliders can at least get away with their sport when safely airborne, since they then take on some element of grace and beauty, the mountain biker will always look a clod.

Part of the cause for derision is the accessories that go with mountain bikes. Everything is day-glo, from pumps and pedals to the funny little helmets the riders wear to stop any further brain damage when they inevitably hit their heads on a rock. Water bottles are sold to clip on the front of the bikes in emulation of the racers in the Tour de France. This is to imply to a bystander that the biker is an athlete in training, with no time to stop and take a drink in a punishing schedule. In fact they spend so much time flying head first into burns, one would have thought they could save even more time by simply opening their mouths and taking on water without the inconvenience of having to reach for the day-glo bottle.

Instead of dressing warmly for the elements, the bikers end up at the summit of popular hills dressed like Paul Weller in a Style Council video. Not only should cycling shorts only be seen on people over six feet tall with perfect bodies, they should never be seen on Ben Lawers in October.

Happily, at the time of going to print the craze is dying a death, as consumers realize that £500 is a lot to pay for something you carry about on one shoulder, and that as a social status symbol it is as impressive as a 1979 Cortina without wheels propped up on bricks.

But since there is obviously a market for the invention of new mountain pursuits, I have been giving it some thought. I am launching my new sport soon in a blaze of publicity. It's called mountain skateboarding. The sports man or woman simply walks to the top of a hill, carrying a special mountain skateboard, and when at the top climbs on the board for a thrill-of-a-lifetime journey down the hill. Already I have been approached by a leading soft drinks manufacturer to host the world mountain skateboarding championships down a terrifying course on Sgurr Alasdair. The skateboards are specially designed for the tough mountain conditions of Scotland, which is why they will retail at £600 each. Well, they're certainly painted pink and say 'mountain' on them in attractive graphics. No doubt you will see an article in *GQ* magazine and *The Face* soon enough. You can say you read about them here first.

Cairn Gorm

Cairn Gorm; 1245m; (OS Sheet 36; 005041); M5.

I DON'T KNOW WHY THE CAIRNGORMS HAVE NEVER turned me on. Maybe it was a reaction to seeing too many Ford Fiestas with back window stickers pleading 'Save The Cairngorms' just above the one with a rainbow saying 'There Is Hope'. Perhaps it could also be blamed on having flicked past hundreds of dull photos of them in *The Scots Magazine* over the years, showing old men with their shirt sleeves rolled up, pointing at some rolling, lumpy, big hills with the caption reading, 'The mighty Cairngorms are a sight for sore eyes in any rambler's book'.

I'm sure the sticker pleading with us to save them is connected with these photos. It's asking us to save them from being depicted in overexposed snaps, and from being constantly pointed at by male senior citizens.

They just didn't seem very exciting. Why would I want to go and wander around on these featureless big sods at

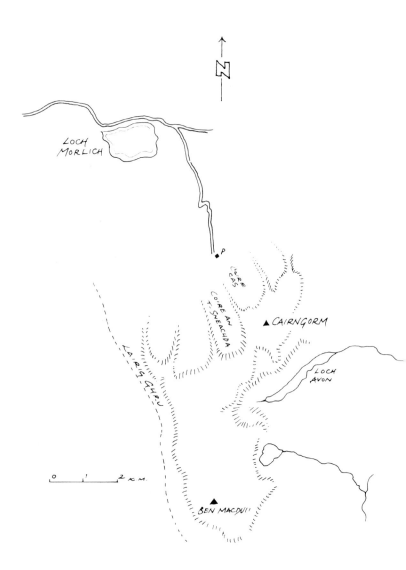

the weekend, when I could be rollicking along a precipice on a terrifying, craggy west-coast mountain? It would be a bit like choosing to go and spend all Sunday afternoon discussing skin diseases with your 75-year-old deaf aunty in Coatbridge, instead of taking up your boyfriend's offer of a day in bed at an expensive country house hotel, drinking champagne while he gives you a bit of a seeing to.

I was a girl who liked my mountains pointy, so I foolishly and ignorantly snubbed the Cairngorms. I was also rather put off by the fact I had inadvertently climbed to the summit of Cairn Gorm from the restaurant at the top of the chairlift one drizzly afternoon years ago. There were lots of people in plastic rain hoods puffing their way up a huge, cobbled stairway, complaining at how wide apart the steps had been laid. It was no fun, and the putrid bridie at the restaurant, thrown across the counter at me by a young waitress who clearly blamed me personally for the shortcomings in her life, was little consolation.

But friends assured me there was more to this grand range of mountains than my experience had suggested, and so to give it a chance I went back to climb Cairn Gorm properly, giving the bridies as wide a body swerve as possible.

The other main obstacle in the way of enjoyment is Aviemore, but unless you need to buy some chips, or have to come by train then you can just close your eyes as you pass by it. Of course this is tricky if you're driving, but ask your passengers to distract you with an Ossianic ballad to keep you from thinking about the importance of Santa Claus Land and The Happy Haggis takeaway to our great Scottish heritage.

Heads should roll for the creation of modern Aviemore, but a public bottom-spanking of the jerks who built it still wouldn't solve the problem of how to get rid of it. The difficulty is that some people actually like Aviemore. Not only do they tolerate the fast-food shops serving up nutriment that top breeders wouldn't recommend for Fido, they go as far as purchasing two expensive weeks in a gruesome timeshare apartment, and sit smoking all day on a balcony overlooking the A9.

It seems also to have a special magnetism for their children, who look forward to spending all day playing video games until it's time to try and get served by a barman who doesn't notice they are 15 and only four feet ten. It was notorious when I was a teenager in Glasgow. For some reason I was unable to fathom, all the girls in my class at secondary school headed for Aviemore each week-end with the singular task of losing their virginity. At least that's how it seemed. They would trip off from school at four o'clock on a Friday, bright-eyed and singing Marc Bolan hits, and return glassy-eyed and forlorn on a Monday, having woken up on Sunday morning in a ditch with a bull-necked squaddie from Preston called Steve, with tobacco breath and boils on his neck. After a few days recovering, they would skip off to get the bus north and have another go. I was bamboozled as to the town's attraction, and I still am. The only positive aspect is that since it attracts the seediest sort of tourist, it keeps them all in one place like a gigantic concrete fly-paper, and stops them wandering all over the unspoiled parts of the Highlands looking for go-cart tracks and timeshare chalets. Yes, I am a snobby old ratbag, and please spell my second name with an A when you write to complain. But I wish I'd been a snobby old ratbag with some power on the Inverness-shire County Council planning committee in the 60s.

Driving to Cairn Gorm is a bit of a cheat, since you drive all the way up to the car park at 640 metres, but then a sea-level start in the Cairngorms is a bit tricky unless you don't mind parking the car in Aberdeen and walking in. Loch Morlich must have been stunningly beautiful once, before the picnic tables and dinghies arrived, and at least the wonderful Scots pines that surround it have survived and are now protected. How I adore Scots pines. There is a modern commercial strain grown for timber that is tall, straight and unremarkable. But these old self-regenerating woods are full of twisted and gnarled specimens, flaunting delightfully shapely canopies, like trees in a 19th-century Japanese silk painting. Who would complain if landowners intent on forestry covered their land with such exotically random foliage instead of the tight rows of lugubrious, tax-avoiding sitkas they are fond of splattering over their hillsides? The Scots pine allows a wealth of wildlife to exist in and under its branches, and it doesn't poke you in the bottom like a sitka if you nip into the woods for a pooh.

There is a splendid view out over this forest of pines from the car park at the base of the Coire Cas chairlift, and it's soothing to be reminded from here how small Aviemore is in the great scheme of things. There is no need to walk up to the summit of Cairn Gorm underneath the chairlift, since there is a route that runs west from the car park, and takes you up on to the Fiacaill ridge, a world away from the frightful clanking kingdom of the ski-tows.

The Fiaca

If only someone would invent ski-tows that could be folded up and packed away after the season. People who both ski and mountaineer, like myself, are fickle creatures. When I go skiing I want dozens of fast tows to whisk me to the top of runs and ensure I don't have to queue for 20 minutes behind a junior racing team, trying to unclip each other's bindings and seeing how far they can spit. But when I pack my skis back into the hall cupboard behind the vacuum cleaner, I want my hills unsullied by pylons and snow fences.

I suppose if I had to make the choice, I would sacrifice skiing for the sake of the hills. After all, skiing in Scotland isn't exactly top class. It usually means clattering over ice and rocks down a three-foot-wide piste, in gale-force winds and horizontal rain. And the après ski is less like a Martini commercial and more like an episode of Colditz. Who would pay a small fortune to come and spend a week in a draughty Highland hotel miles away from the slopes, when they could get a package holiday to somewhere snowy, romantic and convenient in the Alps for half the price? There is nothing uglier than a redundant ski-tow out of season, with its pylons marching up a scarred, broken hillside. The Cairngorm chairlift people are obviously making a great effort to try and limit the damage caused by erosion, by constantly replanting the worn areas with grass seed. But jumbo signs shouting 'Keep Off. Re-seeding in process!' don't do much to help renew the atmosphere of wilderness.

Leave it all behind you and cross the bridge beneath the restaurant that will help you escape south-west towards open country. It's a wonderful surprise to turn the corner, just yards away from the mayhem of the chairlift, and find yourself in wide, sweeping moorland, gently inclining up to the ridge. There are a number of deep paths here, since this is a route to many other peaks and low-level walks, but cross the Allt Coire an t-Sneachda and start to ascend the craggy spur that hugs the western side of the corrie.

My preconceptions about the Cairngorms being dull were shattered by this splendid ridge. The crags along here are heroic, offering sections of exhilarating scrambling if you want to keep to the crest. Down in the corrie, two sparkling blue-green lochans perch beneath the steep cliffs, and it's hard to imagine that just over the next two gullies, people in golf jumpers are tucking into sticky buns. The scale of the boulders is extraordinary, and piles of massive rounded rocks create magical little grottos that beg to have lunch eaten in them. From here you can see the summit of lofty Braeriach to the south-west, iced with a mantle of snow for the majority of the year, and you start to understand what made the old men in shirt sleeves point. I counted myself lucky to be able to see that far, since on this cold October day the weather was starting to turn hostile, with squalls of rain bursting from fast-moving clouds without warning.

It's so irritating having to constantly stop and put your kagoul on, and then stop 40 seconds later to take it off again. How many times have you been walking with someone who does that all the time, regardless of climatic considerations, and wanted to deliver a rabbit punch to the back of their neck when they stop for the tenth time that day and begin the ponderous unclipping of their rucksack? I'm going to work on a revolutionary kagoul that pulls itself on like the hood of a Chevy convertible, and then recedes at the touch of a button. I'll be a millionaire.

After the theatrics of the ridge, it's a strange experience to emerge up on to an enormous flat plateau – a bit like climbing the ladder up to your loft and discovering it leads to an American Football stadium. This is a featureless big plateau, and I arrived on it in a blizzard. It's small wonder that this plateau has claimed lives, since in the weather that I experienced it's impossible to have any sense of direction at all without the constant use of a compass and map. The dangerous thing is that cliffs fall away to the north without warning, and someone getting lost in thick mist could easily come a cropper. The added danger is that turning east instead of west will take a lost party deep into the wild region and away from help, with no prominent features on the hill to help make them realize their error. I was a little unsettled by the fury of the blizzard, and hugged the top of the ridge all the way along, but avoided taking in the top due west of Cairn Gorm in case I was blown off my feet.

Although I left the car park wearing a long-sleeved T-shirt with my warmer clothes packed away in the rucksack, the walk was now a serious business and I was wearing everything I had with me. By the time I stumbled to the summit of Cairn Gorm, it was hard to stand up straight, and the snow driving into my face stung like shotgun pellets. It became important to get off the top quickly. When the weather turns on you like that, you don't have time to stop and curse the fact you're missing the view. All you can do is to keep moving, and hope they still have some bridies in the Ptarmigan restaurant. As soon as I dropped about 70 feet down towards the restaurant, via the tourist runway with its ridiculous little suburban garden fences bordering the steps, the wind ceased and I stepped out of the snow. It's a bit embarrassing to come staggering out of the mist, with a purple face, eyes lost in swollen, battered tissue, gasping for breath, to find people wandering around the path in cardigans and slacks.

The Ptarmigan was closed, and so I walked down beneath the ski-tow towards the road. This is a short-cut walkers are not supposed to take, to prevent erosion, but it would have taken a man with a Rottweiler and a machine-gun to stop me, so desperate was I to get back to the car and home.

I admit I was wrong about the Cairngorms, and I didn't even have the chance to see what was going on behind the plateau to the south. Since I've done most of the really sexy west-coast mountains it's time to start exploring the interior of the Cairngorm range, especially now I've overcome my abhorrence of the ski-tows and scone consumers.

But I draw the line at a car sticker.

Going Into An Outdoor Shop

A S SOON AS YOU HAVE COMPLETED YOUR FIRST hill-walk, a new city hobby opens out to you. You can now go into an outdoor shop. Outdoor shops are just sports shops, but instead of a seedy man with a moustache selling you nylon football strips and tennis balls, outdoor shops stock only merchandise connected with hill-walking, climbing, skiing and sometimes canoeing, all of which will be offered to you by rosy-cheeked young sales people in fleecy tops. Visiting them becomes an addiction. No matter how pressed for time or strapped for cash you may be, should you pass by one of these shops, with a window display of dummies wearing neatly ironed kagouls and ice-axes arranged in a fan shape round a rucksack, you will go inside and not leave until you have purchased a pair of thick socks.

This is mainly the fault of the shop assistants, all of whom climb mountains and will stand discussing Munros with you for 45 minutes, which makes it impossible to leave without buying something. The job of a good outdoor shop sales person is to make the customer feel stupid.

You may have already decided what sort of walking boots to buy, but the shop assistant will, with barely disguised contempt, correct you, telling you how foolish you would have been to buy such footwear, how lucky it was you came here first, and convincing you that for only an extra £65 you can have the boot you really need.

This is not something one would expect in a normal shop. Imagine the newsagent snorting with contempt when you ask for today's *Scotsman*.

'The *Scotsman?*' he would sneer. 'Do you do a lot of newspaper reading, or are you more a weekend reader?'

You would stutter a reply that you just wanted to read some news today.

'Well, fine, if that's what you really want, it's up to you. It's just that most newspaper readers, the serious ones that is, would certainly opt for something a bit thicker, like the *Independent.*'

'Well I'll take an *Independent* then, thanks.'

'Have you read one before?'

'Yes, I think so.'

'Well I'm not keen on selling you one if you're not used to it.'

'No, no, I'm sure I'll be fine. Just give me the *Independent.*'

'Hang on. I'll have to ask the manager.' (Calls to back shop.) 'Joe, there's a grackle in here wants to buy the *Independent*. Have we changed our policy on selling to amateurs?'

(Voice from back shop.) 'Has she bought one before?'

'No, doesn't look like it.'

'OK then, but just this once.'

Of course you wouldn't put up with such nonsense, but you do in an outdoor shop. Just remember that sometimes they can be wrong. I recall going into such a shop a few years ago to replace my survival bag. I fingered a few and then picked out a shiny foil bag that folded neatly down into a tiny pack. At the till the man looked at me and said, 'Used one of these before?'

I replied I had not, since I had been lucky enough so far not to have been forced to fight for my survival. The point, so I thought, was to have one in case of emergency, and hope that it never came out of its pouch.

In that case, he told me with a grim expression, there was something he had to warn me about. I listened intently. These foil bags, unlike the plastic ones, were very dangerous. How could this be, I wondered. Suffocation perhaps, or not enough insulation? He told me. These bags have been known to give people first-degree burns. I stared at the innocent little square of foil on the counter. Yes indeed, he said, the problem is that people just don't realize the incredible temperature of the sun, and how hot a body can get inside one of these things.

I'm sorry to report that I behaved rudely at this point. Throwing my head back and laughing in the man's face was not, on reflection, the correct or polite response. I was not planning a trip to Alice Springs, I pointed out. The survival I had in mind was more huddling with a broken leg under a rock in the snow, trying hard not to die of exposure until some pals bring the Mountain Rescue team.

First-degree burns would seem an unlikely hazard.

'I don't like your attitude,' he informed me, and then went on to say he would feel irresponsible selling me the bag since I displayed such a devil-may-care response to his safety lecture. I bought it regardless, but have been watching ever since for scorch marks on the rucksack pocket where it lives.

At the other end of the scale, good advice in these shops is sometimes very expensive. If you can't afford a new waterproof shell, then don't let an assistant near you. Everything they have in that shop is better than the one you've been wearing for ten years. They will be correct when they explain the advantages of new fabrics, they will also be correct to laugh when you explain what you already use, and you will be bewitched when you try on something fantastic, comfortable and attractive that they slip surreptitiously from a hanger while they talk. But you will be sorry when the Access bill comes in next month if you fall for it.

You'll notice that everything for sale has the capacity to breathe.

'This of course breathes,' the sales person will say, showing you a jacket. 'And the fact that this can breathe makes it all the more comfortable,' they will continue, indicating a hat. When these shops close down for the night, the sound of heavy breathing from their stock must rival that of a porn cinema.

But then grandiose claims are made for most things you can buy connected with mountaineering. My boots are supposed to 'give'. I've had them for over three years now and they haven't remembered a single birthday or Christmas. In fact the only thing they've given me so far are heels like ungrated Parmesan cheese. A shop assistant promised me that a head torch would 'bring me down off the mountain after dark'. Imagine my disappointment when I staggered down a hill in murky twilight after its purchase to find that not only had it been lying in the back seat of the car for the duration of my climb, but that it had failed to come up and get me when the daylight failed.

Of course all this must be much worse if you are a climber rather than a hill-walker. There are only so many things you can sell to someone who merely requires to be kept warm and dry as they walk up a hill. But imagine the delights of selling to a group of people who need serious equipment.

Equipment is a wonderful term. In the vocabulary of people in the retail trade, equipment means wallets being emptied into tills, especially if the purchase of that equipment is the only thing that will ensure they will live to come back and buy more. The climbing section of these shops is bewildering, and is out of bounds to walkers. You may think that in a democracy you too can flick idly through ice-screws and ropes, but the moment you prod anything with an inquisitive finger, an assistant will leap on you with a quiz as to your standard of rock-climbing. The game is up and you must skulk back to your own area, full of socks and thick hats, and leave the mysterious, metallic things to people who can answer such a query with a number and a knowing smile. Don't be too disheartened however. You also leave these people to a rail of hideous nylon tights, with pictures of lions and words like 'climb' in block capitals transferred inexpertly on to the fabric. These are for the climbers, and when you feel puny as a walker you can sidle over to someone looking through this rail and look them straight in the eye, secure in the knowledge that nothing in hill-walking requires you to dress in such a gruesome fashion.

Don't be fooled into thinking that the shop assistants are unconcerned about appearances, that they are just a kooky bunch of crazy kids who live hard, play rough and dress casual. The manager would have had them all in at 8 a.m., forcing them to try on the latest zipper tops over their Iron Maiden T-shirts, and making them practise slouching around the sales floor trying to look cool in clothes designed to save lives in sub-zero temperatures. The customer is supposed to enter the shop, see a young man or woman in a front fastening, reversible, all-weather, windproof, machine-washable smock and think to themselves, 'Hmmm, that guy/chick looks pretty groovy in that smock. Daresay I might splash out and buy one myself.' This is unlikely if those wearing the smocks are in the process of arguing about the lunch-break rota, or sniggering over who will go and frighten away the walker from the climber's rope display.

But these are of course the modern city centre outdoor shops. If you look hard you can still find old shops with window displays like an undertaker's, where a single navy-blue woollen glove on a metal stand would be considered a showy Christmas display. Entering such a store is to enter an intriguing musty lair containing rows of cheap clothes in either blue or olive green, and where you will be greeted by a stab in the eye with an ice-axe that has hung behind the door since the 60s. One might imagine that this is where the real expertise is to be found, where the proprietor might be a famous retired climber scratching a meagre living from the sale of a few anoraks to fuel his or her continuing interest in the hills. In fact it usually turns out to be owned by a used-car dealer and staffed by elderly women who used to work next door at the cake shop and who know as much about mountaineering as goldfish know about pre-Cambrian pottery.

This is the shop that your friends and relations will go to buy you a present. They will not go into the store where the eager young men and women modelling their smocks will sell them something expensive, attractive and useful that you have long tossed and turned at night in the lust to have in your possession. These kindly present-buying people will be set upon immediately by the old cake-shop lady, who will convince them that what all 'the young people' are going for are these lovely olive green PVC capes that fit nicely over a rucksack. Shops like these are the only outlets for such abominations, and the only way you can stop the terrors of opening horrible gifts and feigning delight is to become rich enough to buy them out and turn them into cake shops.

I am considering a helpline for those who simply cannot stop going into outdoor shops and buying aluminium water bottles. I need volunteers to help me man the phones. They will need to have the skills to talk someone out of another pair of loopstitch socks or convince a lost soul that a key-ring with a thermometer measuring wind-chill factor is not going to change their lives. Unfortunately, anyone phoning who wants to buy shiny tights with the word 'climb' on them must be referred to The Samaritans. Some cases are beyond our help.

Beinn Dorain

Beinn Dorain; 1076m; (OS Sheet 50; 326378); M62.

SOME HILLS FORMED AN IMPORTANT PART OF MY childhood. This is not because I climbed them as a child. Far from it. My brother could make me cry just by lifting me on to a five-foot-high garden trellis and leaving me there, so I was hardly a miniature Chris Bonnington. The mountains of my youth were able to influence me only through the back window of a Ford Anglia, as we drove north for camping holidays in the rain. Camping holidays were always in the rain, but my parents would constantly remind us throughout the fortnight that the sun was 'trying to come out'. It was rather disappointing to grow up and find out that the sun didn't give a monkey's testicle whether it came out or not, but was in fact a non-sentient mass of gasses radiating heat and light to earth, except in Scotland.

I kept this news to myself when I found out. We had

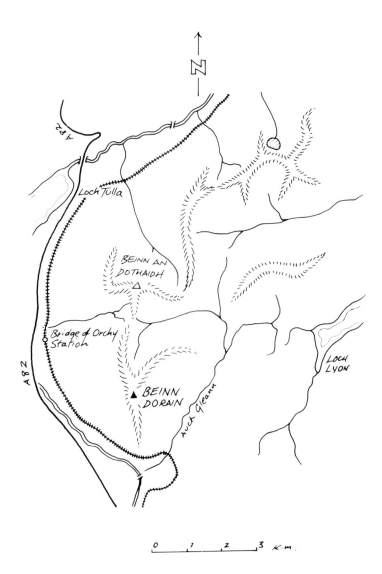

such happy family holidays in the drizzle waiting for the sun to try and come out that it seemed churlish to spoil things with science. I have the sneaking suspicion, fuelled by the clothes they packed, that they knew anyway.

Tempest or not, I was in a constant state of ecstasy, huddled in the back seat between the sleeping-bags and wellingtons, pressing my nose against the steamy window to get a better view of these monsters that disappeared into the mist above us, as we drove to our moist destination. They were full of magic and mystery, even when feeling car sick. To a child, the scale of the mountains is awesome, and I was never convinced that those white dots on the hillside were really sheep. How could anything be that far away? Mind you, I still think that now on the way back from a long hill-walk when I can just make out a dot that is the car.

I desperately wanted to be out there with the sheep, hiding behind boulders and sprinting through the heather. That is until we stopped for a toilet break in a lay-by, when the howling gale and torrential rain lashed our naked bottoms like a Cabinet minister in a Soho sauna, and made me glad to be back in the car beside the sleeping-bags.

One of the mountains that most fascinated was Beinn Dorain. As my father would try in vain to overtake 'a bloody idiot' on the A82 between Tyndrum and Bridge of Orchy, there were two spectacular things to look at before we were wiped out as a family. The first was the incredible viaduct that carried the West Highland railway line over Auch Gleann in an uncompromising, almost perfect horseshoe. The other was the huge and spectacular sweep of Beinn Dorain's west slopes that towered above the railway line giving scale to its forbidding gradient.

We rarely saw its summit, lost as it would be in thick mist, but its mystery made it all the more attractive and seductive. My brother and I would imagine all manner of things to be lurking at the top, from demons' castles to wizards and fairies. Touching to think that as we did so, the reality was probably a few bits of orange peel and a walker in a woollen hat eating a cheese sandwich.

So it was naturally with great affection and nostalgia that as an adult I laced up my boots on a damp October morning at the starting point in the station car park at Bridge of Orchy, in preparation to find out what really lurked at the top of Beinn Dorain. I've always found the settlements on the A82 between Crianlarich and Glencoe most peculiar. Crianlarich, Tyndrum and Bridge

Beinn Dorain

of Orchy are melancholy, stranded little hamlets that
the internal combustion engine has mutated into service
stations for coach parties and crumpled, travel-weary
motorists. A gift shop, a snack bar and a petrol station
is not exactly a model, thriving Highland community,
and the disquieting feeling that these places now exist
only to empty the contents of your wallet if you so much
as slow down is not a pleasant one. Nobody expects
Brigadoon with tartan-skirted villagers singing softly
as they fill your arms with sweet heather and invite
you in to their fireside. But we could all do with a
few less stuffed velvet Loch Ness monsters and dismal
cafeterias that smell of incontinence.

However, Bridge of Orchy station is a very convenient
starting point, and after crossing beneath the railway line
a prominent path leads you up the hill in the direction
of a gully that divides Beinn Dorain from its sister Munro,
Beinn an Dothaidh. It goes without saying, unless you're a
reader with severe learning difficulties, that this is a corker
of a hill to do if you don't have a car. The West Highland
line from Glasgow runs regularly and you can easily plan
a day by the train timetable, unless of course you live in
Ullapool. However, the Conservative Government, at the
time of writing, are trying in the most unsubtle ways to
destroy the rail network in Scotland, a crime that gener-
ations to come will curse them for if they succeed. When
I first started to explore Scotland by train, there were long
spacious carriages, first and second class, with a restaurant
and buffet, a guard's van where bikes could be carried
free of charge, and a service that transported you to the
Highlands through snow drifts that would bury a car.

Now there are two-carriage abominations called 'Sprinters' that are so basic and degrading a form of transport for a long journey that adequate toilet facilities are considered an unnecessary luxury. Scotrail cannot be so terminally stupid that they are unaware of the numbers of people wanting to use the train in the summer, and therefore a train that accommodates more than four people at a time may well be required. So one is forced to conclude that the reason hundreds of dismayed tourists and walkers are stranded on stations up and down the length of the West Highland line at the height of the season, unable to squeeze into an already packed 'Sprinter', if it arrives at all, is that somebody is doing this on purpose. The thought of all the ingenuity and hard Scottish toil spent on the line's construction being deliberately discarded by a bunch of greedy, sly, ignorant English Conservatives in London that nobody up here voted for makes my rage barely containable.

Sorry. Back to the hill.

The path up the gully from Bridge of Orchy is certainly the shortest route to the two peaks, but for a longer and more spectacular walk there is a deliciously tempting circuit round the back of the mountains via Auch Gleann. The beauty of that trail is that you have the thrill of walking beneath the railway viaduct and carrying on up alongside the Allt Chonoghlais into Coire a' Ghabhalach, the mirror eastern corrie of the one gained by the Bridge of Orchy route. A route not to take unless you know no fear, is to walk straight up the sweeping southern flanks of the hill, which will leave you giddy and hanging on to craggy, near-vertical terrain with your teeth. The sweeping contours of the hill at that point have always reminded me of a huge wave about to break, and it's an uncomfortable thought trying to imagine where you might stop for lunch, and what would happen if you dropped your orange. But by walking up to the eastern corrie, Coire an Dothaidh, fear is not an issue; only leg muscle. It's a fast ascent on to the bealach, and then a right turn takes you on to a surprising flat little plateau sporting a tiny circular lochan.

In accordance with my usual run of luck, I climbed up into thick mist, and being too lazy and smug to take a bearing I followed what seemed to be a well-worn path heading in the right direction for Beinn Dorain. The mist looked as though it had been created by the BBC special effects department for a studio play about Jack the Ripper, and yards away I could hear voices without being able to see the humans making the sound. It's a strange voyeuristic sensation to hear people talking when they have no idea you are there, and the temptation is strong to make frightening bellowing noises and then hide behind a rock. This party, oblivious to my presence, were arguing over whether or not they had found the summit, which depressed me somewhat. The Scottish Mountaineering Club's Munros book had warned of a false summit cairn, and if I had longed to see the view from Beinn Dorain, and look down on that road from which the young Gray had gazed upwards 25 years ago, I was going to be disappointed unless the mist lifted. Following the path with my thoughts wallowing in nostalgia, I soon found myself back where I started and crashing into the people I had heard through the mist. Since they hadn't spotted me earlier, there was no embarrassment attached to my circuitous ramble and I hailed them with a tone of voice that sounded as if I knew what I was doing.

They asked me if this was the way down, which given my navigational skills thus far was a bit like asking a page three girl to compare Bertold Brecht with Harold Pinter. I said I believed them to be following the correct route and then crept off into the mist surreptitiously to whip out my compass. I found the deceptive cairn and followed the instructions to find the real summit over a slight drop in the ridge. However, it barely mattered if this was the summit or not since the view barely extended to my feet. It's at such times, as you sit eating a damp sandwich as water drips from your nose, as you scour the map for all the things you can't see, that you wonder why the hell you do it. But then the majority of hill-walking is done in less than satisfactory weather, and somehow, no matter how foul and inclement it is, you cannot wait to get back up the hills and do it again. Sometimes, when a party of you are trudging through boggy ground, battered by wind and rain, you catch somebody's eye and the whole thing seems ludicrous. I can't begin to explain why such a pursuit should be enjoyable. Perhaps it's the moaning you can do at the top, or the relief of getting down and into the warmth. Whatever the reason, you will have to take my word for it that a hill-walk is still an exhilarating day out even when you can't see a thing.

Some of the things I couldn't see included Loch Lyon to the east with Ben Lawers beyond, Ben More to the south, Ben Lui to the south-west and lovely Glen Orchy to the west leading to Ben Cruachan.

Some of the things I could see were some sheep droppings, a stone or two, my rucksack and an aluminium
ring pull from someone's can of juice.

So I headed back, realizing that plans to combine Beinn
an Dothaidh should be abandoned since the view would be
remarkably similar from its summit, although it might
not boast a ring pull.

Mist is a swine, and on arriving back at the little lochan
I started to become confused again. I dropped down from
the loch only to find that the terrain was considerably
steeper than I recalled on the way up, although the
compass said I was doing fine. The last thing I wanted
was to find myself slithering down the steep craggy
section above the corrie, having mistakenly bypassed the
Y-shaped gully that led back to the car, yet I could sense
I was getting it all a bit wrong. Then I heard voices. The
same party of people I had encountered earlier were still
sitting having lunch on the edge of some rocks above me.
There was nothing for it. I was now going to have to
ask them if this was the way down. This was not how
I had imagined the conquering of my childhood dream
peak, and I was muttering and tutting under my breath
as I clambered up towards them.

They looked expectantly towards me.

'Excuse me,' I said in as casual a voice as I could muster,
and as the words left my lips a strange and wonderful
thing happened. Below me the clouds parted with alarming speed, revealing the glen below in astonishing clarity.
So dramatic was its timing and swiftness I paused to see
if angels with trumpets would slide into view with some
glad tidings. I could see the railway line, the road, Bridge

of Orchy, and practically read the tax disc on my car. I was standing in absolutely the correct place for my descent.

Then I remembered the party of walkers above me.

'Could you tell me the time please?' I said, completing my unfinished enquiry. Asking the way down with the glory of sight restored would have been stupid in the extreme, and I gave secret thanks for my ego salvation. I was told it was 2.30 and I started home without blushing.

I wonder if there really are time traps, where events and people from the past remain locked in a moment that can be revisited by those in the future. If so, it would have been splendid to have seen a small blue Ford Anglia spluttering along the road as I descended, with a tiny white face peering from a condensation-covered back window. I would have waved happily but kept the secret of the summit to myself. No demon's castle, no wizards or fairies. Just a wet walker in a woollen hat, eating a cheese sandwich in the rain.

What's In Your Rucksack?

I'VE OFTEN BEEN ASKED, 'WHAT'S IN YOUR RUCK-sack?' Mind you, I've been coming back through customs at Heathrow at the time, wearing an old leather jacket and twitching with a wildly suspicious glint in my eye, so perhaps there was good reason. But the contents of your backpack are all-important and should be regularly scrutinized to assess their effectiveness, and also to make sure you haven't left a pork pie in there from last July.

Food is obviously the first item on your rucksack checking agenda, and it astonishes me that some people actually take to the hills without any food at all. I can't get up the first 100 feet of a hill-walk without having to cram chocolate into my face, so heaven knows how someone can fast all day on a long ridge-walk without passing out. It also has such a keen psychological effect on a walk, giving tired walkers something to look forward to at the top, that I wonder what spurs on those who are without a sandwich. Incidentally, perhaps one of the rudest things a hill-walker can do when out on the hills with companions is to eat their lunch before reaching the summit. Not only do all the others have to stop and wait while this thoughtless hog tucks into his or her Tupperware box, but the question arises in everyone's mind, where is this person going to get more food from when they find themselves at the top, inevitably hungry again? The answer is that they will eat some of your lunch. Either such people are born survivors, stoking up with everyone else's rations in case of an emergency, or they're just rude, greedy bastards.

Whatever the reason, never go hill-walking with anyone again if they lunch at a different time from the rest of the group. This goes for opening cans of juice too. Cans of juice on hill-walks are there to be opened at lunch-time and handed round. Never let the slowest person have the rucksack with the canned juice in it. Leave them with their own water bottle or you'll find that on a triumphant conquering of the top, all there is left to celebrate with is a rucksack full of empty Fanta cans.

People's lunch habits tell you a great deal about them. I've always felt a little queasy about those who wrap their sandwiches in the bag the bread came in. I can't explain what seems to be so unpleasant about a person eating out of a greaseproof paper bag that reads 'Sunblest', but it conjures up the atmosphere of squalid Sunday School picnics that had to be moved indoors to a church hall with strip lights because of rain.

Then there are those who wrap sanwiches in tin foil. I knew someone who continually rolled his used foil into a large cumulative ball each time he finished his sandwiches, keeping the big silver ball 'handy' in his rucksack. The consequences of sheltering with him from a thunder-storm at lunchtime don't bear thinking about. Climbers and walkers whose mother has a hand in packing their lunch may be familiar with the maternal method of individually wrapping each sandwich in tight clingfilm. While keeping the sandwiches fresh and clean through-out the walk, the diner unfortunately is still struggling to unwrap the first cheese roll while everybody else is smacking their lips and making ready to move off after a hearty meal. The best sandwich storing method is of course Tupperware. Unfortunately this renders the image of the walker somewhat less than macho, since Tupperware doesn't exactly have the call of the wild about it. One can't imagine Shackleton crawling through the snow and stopping to get the Tupperware. In fact the account of his incredible polar expedition, that forced him over the massive mountains of South Georgia to the safety of the whaling station at Stromness Bay, recalls that all he had to eat were some dry biscuits wrapped in a sock. However, it has to be said that wrapping your lunch in a sock is still better than a Sunblest bag. Tupperware could improve their marketability with mountaineers overnight by going into partnership with one of the big outdoor equipment manufacturers like Berghaus. They could then produce suitably manly Tupperware, perhaps with an individual corporate brand name like 'Ascent Storm Force Eat-ware'. With only a simple design adjustment, they could manufacture the boxes in red, blue and olive green, print a graphic of a snow-covered peak on the lids, and they'd be battering them off the production line faster than the Royal Family can breed. With such an image, even the most hairy and burly of mountaineers could get clean away with fishing out the Tupperware.

'Is that a Tupperware box you have there, Tom?'

'Don't be daft, Sandy. This is that new Ascent Storm Force Eat-Ware. Real state of the art technology, this.'

'Oh yeah. Think I read about it in *Climber* magazine. Is that the stuff tested by astronauts?'

'Yeah, too right it is. Specially designed to withstand the most severe conditions the human body can tolerate, at fantastic altitudes. Do you fancy a bit of this aubergine and parsley quiche?'

But Tupperware is only for the most organized of walkers. The advent of pre-packed sandwiches and fizzy drinks on sale at petrol stations has turned a lot of us who have cars into slobs. Instead of having to get up at 6 a.m. to heat up the soup and make the sandwiches, you can roll out of bed half an hour later and pick something up when you stop to fill up the tank. The problem is you can get caught out that way and arrive at the filling station to find no sandwiches, nor anything faintly resembling lunch. Somehow a bag of winegums, a Twix and some marshmallows don't hit the spot at the cairn the way only a chicken tikka and lettuce sandwich can. It's just that preparing the food in the morning is such a hideous task. The chances are, if it's a Saturday morning, you were out on the town the night before and decided at one in the morning on the way home from a club with friends that it would be great to do The Five Sisters tomorrow. Facing salami and ploughman's pickle first thing next morning is not a great way to start the day, and it doesn't get any better when the only soup you can find in the cupboard is lobster bisque.

The only thing worse than packing a rucksack first thing in the morning is unpacking it completely once a year to springclean it. I will lay good money on the bet that nobody has escaped the flat Mars Bar. This is a completely flat confectionery that is roughly the size and shape of a business envelope, with a wrapping so crackled and faded that it is hard to make out what the black and red markings could mean. The flat Mars Bar indicates that there are parts of your rucksack that have not been explored for some time, and is a timely and poignant reminder of many happy days in the hills. This amazing creation started life as a normal, three-dimensional chocolate block, placed carefully at the top of the backpack, handy to get at when the need for instant energy arose. On its first outing, it was pushed to the bottom of the pack by a kagoul being lifted roughly out and replaced without thought to the chocolate bar now relegated to the very bottom of the rucksack. There is, like Dante's vision of Hell, no escape for a chocolate bar dropped to the bottom of the rucksack, and as it falls into the abyss past a long-forgotten hat, it can read 'Abandon hope all who enter here' inscribed on the Gortex lining. Many months of being sat on, thrown in and out of car boots and being stood on at cairns will work like a cobbler at an anvil on the Mars Bar, until the final perfectly flat shape we all know so well is achieved. How often I have wondered if during a life or death situation, I would have the courage to search for, locate and eat my flat Mars Bar. I hope it is a test I will never have to endure.

Indeed rucksacks seem to be designed to conceal their contents, rather than present them usefully when required, and I appear to have pockets on mine that I haven't put my hand into for years. While groping about for a camera recently, I came across a pouch with zipper I had no idea existed. With breathless excitement I unzipped it to see what treasure lay there. It contained some broken red boot laces, an empty raisin box and some hair grips. I can't ever recall taking hair grips with me on a hill-walk, but the pouch said different. When I see children's programmes like *Blue Peter* burying capsules full of 20th-century artifacts for future archaeologists to dig up, I feel like writing in and volunteering to put it in my rucksack. It has less chance of being uncovered there than in the ground.

Which brings me to the choice of the rucksack itself. This is more than just a vital part of the climber and hill-walker's equipment. It is a life-style statement. Every shop selling rucksacks displays dazzling coloured examples in every size and shape. And yet out on the hill there are still people walking around with dark-green self-coloured rucksacks. It must take enormous strength of character to fly in the face of peppermint green, fuchsia and sunshine-yellow rucksacks, and actually sign the cheque for one in dark green. I take my hat off to such people, although I wouldn't like to spend the night in a bothy with them.

Having chosen the sack, it's time to decide how to wear it, and what to have hanging from it. The things that swing from your rucksack are as important as what rides inside. Climbers show the world they are more than just pansy hill-walkers by covering their rucksacks with ropes, metal things and more metal things. A keen hill-walker will have an ice-axe and crampons dangling from their rucksack for most of the year (until somebody in Raybans, shorts and a T-shirt laughs at them), and it's important how and where you attach this ice-axe, since an inexpertly dangled implement can end up swinging loose into your bottom with alarming momentum. Most good rucksacks will have special loops to fit the axe, but if, like me, your rucksack was designed in 1952 to take some quail's eggs and a pair of gloves, then you will end up being creative with the straps. The worst thing you can do is to attach the shaft of the ice-axe to something stable and the pick end of it to something that may give way. That's a recipe for Mountain Rescue turning up to find you impaled to a memorial cairn in the most unbecoming fashion. The best policy is to carry it like a walking stick. If it's cold and icy enough to need one, then you should have it out all the time anyway, but it does rather leave you wondering what else you can hang from the rucksack. Try animal skulls. At least you'll get a space to yourself at the cairn.

Packing the rucksack is an art, and a friend of mine always packs his to capacity, even on a two-hour walk. He takes a complete change of clothing, a sleeping-bag and ground mat, food for two days, a head torch, compass, spare laces and a small stove for emergency cooking. This may seem excessive, but then this was a man who, through a grave time miscalculation, became 'be-nighted' on Liatach. His frequency in recounting the tale of being 'be-nighted' prompted his friends to call him Sir Peter. This is a cautionary tale in the use of mountain-speak. Never say 'be-nighted' – just say you got caught overnight on the hill. However, Sir Peter will want for nothing if it happens to him again, since he carries more creature comforts in his rucksack than I have in my house.

So if you have time to spare, remember that the packing and stocking of the rucksack is all-important in preparing for that expedition into the hills. Slothfulness may overwhelm you, and you may want to stay up and watch a Chilean film on Channel 4 until two in the morning, but believe me you will regret it the next day if that rucksack is still unpacked and neglected.

There is, of course, a general rule you can follow to ensure that your rucksack is always well stocked, ready for action, with delicious sandwiches packed in Tupperware boxes, clean and tidy, and with no nasty surprises lurking in any of the pockets. Marry someone rich and get Filipino help.

Filming the Munros

I's A MISTAKE TO FOLLOW MY ADVICE, FOR THE simple reason that I never follow it myself. When a young TV researcher I was working with asked me which sort of programme they should work on next, I furrowed my brow, leant over and wagged a finger. 'Never . . .' I said sagely, fixing their astonished gaze, '. . . never, ever work on a programme about something you love doing in your spare time. You will grow to loathe your own hobby.'

A year later I was heaving myself up An Teallach with a film crew, making *The Munro Show* for Scottish Television.

So I was wrong. Filming the Munros didn't make me hate them, but it did give me the opportunity to nearly wipe out a team of six people.

It started when I foolishly mentioned to Alastair Moffat at Scottish that I was in the middle of writing a book about Munros. He was looking for an outdoor series, and since I was already bathed in the sweat of mountain fever I rashly suggested putting together a programme based on some of the subjects I had been scribbling about. This was not a particularly sensible idea at the time. There were very good reasons why nobody had done a regular, magazine-format hill-walking programme before, not least the fact that film crews can rarely be persuaded to walk more than 50 yards from their car, and start to whine and paw the director if they can't break for a pub lunch at 1 p.m. sharp. I was going to have to ask a crew to strap equipment to their backs, climb 12 mountains over 3,000 feet, and think themselves lucky if they managed a ten-minute break for a sandwich at the top.

Far be it for me to mention that there had been certain other programmes where some cheating had gone on, by flying film crews to the tops of hills in helicopters and pretending they had hoofed it. This certainly would not do for *The Munro Show.* Not just because of the underhand deception, but because to spend the latter part of the summer out walking the hills and be paid for it seemed too good a chance to miss. We knew we would have to use a helicopter to get high dramatic shots to cut in with the bulk of the programme, but everyone agreed the only way to make it work would be to climb the mountains first, in exactly the way a normal hill-walker would.

Assembling the crew was like asking for volunteers to join a chain gang, yet we had everybody in under a week. Alasdair Walker, the cameraman, was already a keen hill-walker, sound man Brian Howell wasn't but was keen to try, Ross Murray, the researcher, was a bearded rock-climber who had done well over 100 Munros, Angus Lamont, the associate producer, said he didn't mind a standard ten-hour day in the wilds, although he rolled his eyes when he said it, and Vivien Robertson, the production manager, who would normally expect to be in a cosy office with a fan heater under the desk, found herself heaving camera batteries up mountains before she could get to a phone and call her union. With three willing, interchangeable runners, Rod, Ronnie and Fraser, the mountain team was complete.

When you have a crew that will go anywhere, the opportunities are huge, and so we chose the hardest and most dramatic hills we could think of to make the series spectacular. The problem was we couldn't start filming until halfway through August. Any hill-walker knows that not only does the weather start to deteriorate precisely at this time, but the men with rifles are polishing their barrels and dusting down their plus fours for the impending deer-stalking season. Not a great time to start a series about mountains, but we had no choice. How was I to know we would come a cropper on a fairly regular basis? My lawyers are working on some plausible excuses.

THE AONACH EAGACH

At least we started filming without too many traumas, other than blisters the size of fried eggs on the long walk back out of Creag Meagaidh, but when the stalking season got underway we were struggling with access problems. So in mid-September we headed for Glencoe to do the Aonach Eagach ridge, since The National Trust for Scotland who own it allow access all year round. It's

almost worth buying one of their bookmarks with baby
owls on them at their visitor centre, just to say thank
you. No, come to think of it, that's asking a bit too much.
On arrival, however, Glencoe was under a characteristic
downpour. Our hearts sank. The weather forecast said
the West of Scotland should have cleared by 10 a.m.,
but nobody had told Glencoe. We hung around miserably
in the Clachaig eating gargantuan quantities of cheese
toasties until we felt sick. In such situations everybody
tries to look busy. Vivien always has calls to make, Ali and
Brian can fiddle with screwdrivers and lens cloths, and I
try and look like a producer doing some work by opening
my big folder and laying it out on the table. Nobody is
ever fooled by this device, since all I do is put my coffee
on top of it and stare vacantly into space for two hours.
Then suddenly, at noon the clouds began to lift.

Making a programme up a mountain is quite different
to hill-walking for fun. Every time I decide I want to say
something to camera it takes on average half an hour to get
all the equipment out, perform the piece and then pack
it all back up again. If I'm in usual form, which means 15
takes just to remember which mountain we're on, then it
can take considerably longer. So knowing that we couldn't
possibly start and finish the ridge in so short a time with
those difficulties in mind, it was agreed that a walk to the
top of Am Bodach would do for the day. We would have
to come back and complete the ridge when the weather
improved. At least that was the plan. Sunset was at 8.30
p.m. that day and it seemed like a long way off.

At 2 p.m. we started up the steep path to Am Bodach
at the east end of the ridge. Ali Walker had purchased

a rucksack that would take the awkward bulk of his camera, and although it weighed more than any of us would care to carry across a room without having to sit down, he was always miles ahead on every walk. This, quite naturally, was a source of some irritation. Every other outdoor programme appears to make a big deal of how 'the crew are carrying such heavy equipment, they'll be continuing by Land-Rover while we walk over the top and meet them'. So it was rather annoying when the crew carrying the heavy stuff kept a constant 20 yards in front of the presenter carrying only her sandwiches and a hat. I resolved to give them all a bit of a talking to later, but the weather was spectacular by the time I caught up with Ali to do the first link, at a dramatic spur of rock called The Chancellor. The views down Glencoe from here are fabulous, and after a morning of torrential rain, with a cloud level of about four feet, the glistening sunlit rocks on Bidean Nam Bian, the warmth of the sun and the azure blue sky acted on our spirits like a drug. It's this elated part of the day I blame for what happened later. We carried on up to Am Bodach, where the vista across to Ben Nevis and the Mamores was breathtaking. We stopped and had a conference about what to do.

The Aonach Eagach is mainland Britain's narrowest ridge, a walk between two Munros, Meall Dearg and Sgorr Nam Fiannaidh, and for someone like me who suffers from vertigo, it's a brown underpants job.

If doing the walk from east to west, it's at Am Bodach you have to make the decision to go down or carry right along to the end, since once on the ridge there's no way off until you reach the second Munro. Researcher

Ross looked at his watch and said we'd never make it now, and we should probably go back. But the sun was beating down, the visibility was incredible and the hills of Scotland had never looked more beautiful. We all shouted at him in derision and decided to carry on, but Ross was not a happy man.

The first bit of scrambling occurs just after Am Bodach, and takes you up to Meall Dearg. It was horrible. However, nobody else seemed to be suffering, and every time I looked round for support they were chatting to each other with their hands in their pockets about whether we should stop off later for a curry in Fort William. I started to feel a little hard done by. Others could get away with being frightened in privacy, whereas my yellow streak was to be recorded for a few million people to share and snigger at. We carried on to the narrowest section of the ridge, where some careful navigation round a pinnacle is required to reach the safety of a wider path and where the feeling of exposure is tremendous. I wanted this filmed as it happened, so the crew crossed first and set up, leaving me behind to climb across towards them when they were ready. So cowardly was I, however, that I made Ross hide behind bits of rock just in front of me, to whisper where I should put my feet. Pathetic I know, but you have no idea how comforting it is having someone with a beard in front of you hissing, 'Psst . . . foothold to the left!'

The trouble is that all this trauma took a great deal of time, even though we were practically running between the scrambling sections, and by the time we reached the second Munro it was 8 p.m.

The sun was setting over the sea and I have never seen anything so spectacular. Ali the cameraman agreed, and while Ross danced around, frothing at the mouth and pointing at his watch, we were taking shot after shot of the mountains fading through purples and pinks into a glorious dusk. Mountaineers among you will quickly deduce that if we were filming the sun setting from the last Munro, it would have gone completely by the time we were ready to descend. You would be right. We had planned to come down safely on the north side of the ridge, beside the pap of Glencoe, but after a hurried conference we decided to attempt a descent by the terrifying path above the Clachaig which the Scottish Mountaineering Club book strongly advises against, even in daylight. It would save us valuable time, and although dangerous the general opinion was that stumbling down the heathery slopes to the north in the dark, without benefit of a clear path, would mean a broken leg every hundred yards.

It was totally dark when we gained the upper reaches of the path, and I buckle under the embarrassment that not one of us had a head torch. Never, under any circumstances, attempt to descend that path in the dark. In fact, never under any circumstances attempt to descend it at all. Every rock is loose, and the gradient is so severe that the lights of the Clachaig could be seen between our feet as we stumbled down like toddlers looking for their mum. We were totally silent as we picked a way through the black night, with the sounds of revelry in the bar below drifting up to us, torturing us in our plight. Each step knocked another boulder down into the inky abyss below and possibly on to somebody's head, and there was little energy left to deal with this last and most dangerous hurdle. Everyone was practically dead on their feet, and apart from the regular shouts of 'below!' and 'aaaargh . . . a rock!' only Ross had enough energy to say anything, which was a series of variations on 'I told you so'. It was so dark nobody could see each other, and we could only trust we still had a complete party by the sounds of people whimpering nearby. The only way to navigate was by the luminescence of white rocks on the path.

We burst into the Clachaig at 10.30 p.m., just as the manager's fingers twitched on the phone dial to call out Mountain Rescue. Imagine how humiliating it would have been to have a rescue team come and fetch a film crew making a programme about how to tackle the Munros. We muttered about why we were so late and stuck our red and sheepish faces into some beer glasses to consume the most welcome pints imaginable. It was a miracle nobody was hurt and I resolved it would never happen again. Well at least that was the best-laid plan, but you know what Burns said about those.

THE IN PIN

Skye is not exactly famous for a Mediterranean climate, so I can't imagine why we were surprised to find it cold, wet and miserable on arrival. We had come to film the ultimate Munro, Sgurr Dearg, known to those who quake in their walking boots at the thought of rock-climbing as the Inaccessible Pinnacle, but it's not a task that can be contemplated in high winds and torrential rain. At this point in the shoot we were so familiar with the weather forecast that we shouted about isobars and depressions in our sleep, but the tiny regional variations can make the difference between being able to climb and film, or not being able to get out of the car.

The Met Office promised two clear days and we planned an early start to take advantage of them the very next day. After our Aonach Eagach experience, we had invested in head torches and made a strict rule about when we should leave the summit. This was later still in the season, and sunset was around 7.30, so Ross demanded assurance that we would leave no later than 6 p.m. from the base of the In Pin to make our descent. It was a deal. Nobody wanted another night hike. We set off early from the Glen Brittle Memorial hut and made good progress up on to the ridge that leads to Sgurr Dearg. It was slightly overcast, but the cloud level was high above the peaks and there was no wind, so the only worry for me was whether I would see my breakfast again when I stood in front of the climb. Although Sgurr Dearg is not a particularly high Munro, at only 986 metres, the going is tough and I was puggled as well as petrified when at last we stood beneath that terrifying blade of rock that is the In Pin.

We were to be disappointed. From nowhere, a mist swirled in and obscured the summit, but more perilously, left the rock too wet and slippery to climb safely. The more usual way to the top for Munroists is by the long sloping fin of the rock on its southerly side, where the ascent is no more than an exposed scramble. But we were going for a climb up the vertical north face for two

The film crew. From left to right: Angus Lamont, Vivien Robertson, the

uthor and Alasdair Walker. Crouching: Brian Howell and Ross Murray

reasons. Firstly, that it would make better TV, and secondly Ross pointed out that for a first-time rock-climber
like me, it was safer to be on a vertical climb where a
fall would mean a dangle straight down on a few feet of
tight rope, instead of a huge, dangerous pendulum swung
over the longer side. I suspected the real reason was Ross
wanting vengeance for an entire summer of jokes about
his beard, but I kept my fears to myself.

With the summit still in cloud at 5.30, the day was
useless and we skulked off down to a horrible dinner in
a grim Skye hotel. We had a rule that we didn't climb
two days in a row, to save people's leg muscles and stop
a full-scale mutiny erupting. But we awoke the next day
to the news that the weather was going to improve from
early afternoon, so we broke our own code and headed
back up the mountain to have another go.

All the way up the sun shone and light clouds scur-
ried across the sky. From the ridge the walker can look
across Coire Lagan and see the magnificent scree slopes
of the mighty Sgurr Alasdair, a sight that requires the
viewer to plunder their own thesaurus for adjectives to
describe its beauty. Coire Lagan is a wonderful sight
as it cradles a blue-green lochan in its arms and is
ringed by ferocious grey cliffs, and the scale of Sgurr
Alasdair perceived from high above the corrie on the
Sgurr Dearg ridge is unnerving. The ridge also offers
views across the sea to the islands of Rhum, Eigg, Canna
and Soay, and it was notable that climbing it a second
day made none of these features any less enthralling.

The Cuillins of Skye are quite unlike anywhere else
in Scotland, and depending on the weather they appear

as if part of a desperate barren moonscape or take on an Alpine grandeur. They couldn't quite make up their mind that day, and swung from being dark and demonic one moment, to sunlit and genial the next. When we arrived at the base of the In Pin, with the second day's climb taking its toll on energy and good humour, the summit was clear. Unfortunately a party of climbers were in the process of making their way to the top along the long southerly side, so we were required to wait for them to complete their climb and abseil down. My nerves were on edge as I realized that it had to be today or never. Would it be easy like Ross said? Would I fall off and die? Could I make the abseil down without crying? At least I was going to see some people doing it properly before we had to give it a go. That, I was sure, would put my mind at ease.

Half an hour later we were watching with our mouths open as a girl on the summit was lowered down from the top on a rope like a sack of potatoes, whacking her face against the rock as her hands were busy high above her head holding on to her lifeline. Cruelly hilarious as it was, I nearly fainted. That would be me. I would have to be lowered down like that, and I would never put a kagoul on again. Oh the shame, the terror, the panic.

What I should have been worrying about was the time. As the last of the unfortunate potato woman's party hopped down from the top, God decided we should suffer a little more, and a massive front of cloud swept in and once again obscured the top. This time we waited. We had little choice. There was no way at all we could come back again the next day, since our schedule was already miles out. If we didn't climb it that afternoon, we would have to drop it from the programme. We waited until 5.30, when Ross looked at his watch and said it was nearly time to get moving, but we had seen little breaks in the cloud so we stayed put. At 5.45 a substantial break in the clouds appeared and revealed the top to us again. The rock was dry, the hole in the clouds looked like it might last for half an hour, so we leapt to it. Once again, Ross was not a happy man.

Ross went up first, with nothing to stop him falling off and mashing himself on the hard rock except balance, nerve and leg muscles like tights stuffed with grapefruits.

In all the things I have been required to do in the line of television duty I have never been more genuinely terrified. Brian fitted Ross and I with personal radio mikes since his boom, the furry microphone on a stick you see sound men waving at politicians outside court rooms, would never pick up our words from such a distance. The result was not a lively conversation between Ross and I as we merrily claimed the summit, but a tape full of me making noises like a cat in a liquidiser, while Ross bellowed at me from above. Later in the editing suite, I had to remove most of the sound from the pictures because of my hideously sharp breathing, whimpering and swearing. It doesn't take much to make you forget you're supposed to be presenting a television programme, and as soon as I started to climb I was oblivious to everything except the 3,000-foot drop and the fact that I couldn't find anything to hold on to.

But we did it, and as I abseiled down there wasn't a happier woman in Scotland. It was now nearly 6.30 p.m.

and the cloud was starting to thicken again. We knew it was late, but Ali and Angus wanted to climb to the top. Since they had come this far twice in two days it seemed unfair to say no, so Ross went back up and let the pair of them take their turn. Yes, thank you, readers, I know how stupid this seems to you as you sit tutting at this folly from the safety of a comfy chair, but it didn't feel so outrageous at the time. It was 7 p.m. when we started to descend, and we knew if we made it down off the ridge on to the lower grassy slopes by 7.45, we would be fine. Sadly the mist decided to audition for a part in a horror movie, and before we reached the crucial turning on the ridge that led down on to the plateau, visibility was down to about 20 feet.

We made an error. For some reason we turned and headed south, missing the gap in the rocks that we needed to find, and headed downhill, totally unaware we were heading for the cliffs above Coire Lagan. As it grew darker, the way became more impassable, until we were hanging on to a cliff by our fingertips in near blackness. The compass wouldn't work on these magnetic rocks, and we had no idea what lay below us. When somebody dislodged a rock with their feet and it fell for an uncomfortably long time in silence before smashing apart hundreds of feet below, we knew we were in trouble. Ross made our choice clear. We would have to climb all the way back up on to the ridge if we were to have any chance of finding the path. It was either that or we stayed put and spent the night on the mountain. Nobody was keen on the second option, so we retraced our steps as best we could and regained the ridge. By a huge stroke of luck, we found the path as the very last milky drops of light faded from the mist. Once again it was a descent in complete darkness, aided by three head torches among seven. I had left mine in my car.

The scramble down the rocks to the safety of the grass was something nobody will forget, or indeed let me forget when I ask them to work with me again. People fell every few minutes, tripping and stumbling through exhaustion and blindness, and on reaching the grassy slopes below the crags, trips had turned into full-scale, head-first tumbles into the heather. Nobody got back to the car without having partaken in amateur acrobatics that resulted in a face full of peat.

As we sat over some soup at the Sligachan Hotel at quarter to eleven at night, the crew glaring at me with naked accusation in their eyes, I fought back the tears and a genuine regret that I had not gone to Scottish Television with an idea for a chat show in a warm studio. Cheating has a lot to offer.

HELICOPTER PHOBIA

After every climb, we needed to return to the mountain on a completely separate day, drop me at the places I had delivered my pieces to camera, film it and try and cut it all together as if it happened at the same time. The difficulties in that plan are enormous, not least that Scotland rarely offers two days of weather alike. The difficulty for me was that I had to jump in and out of a helicopter that was not always able to make a completely stable landing on two runners, on top of terrifying ridges and peaks.

Dominic, our pilot from PLM Helicopters, gave me a brief safety rundown pointing out with some glee all the things that could go wrong, and reminding me that it was at my own risk. As an afterthought he added, 'Oh, and try to remember not to run downhill at me to get back in. You'll probably decapitate yourself.'

I was hardly likely to forget. In fact I tossed and turned at night thinking of the bill PLM would land us with for clogging up their blades with bits of my face.

But who could complain about flying all over Scotland's mountains, leaping in and out at all the most exciting places on a hill? There was one factor, however, that drove me wild with rage. Every time we returned to a hill with the helicopter and dropped me at the summit, there were always two or three walkers sitting at the cairn, watching the proceedings sardonically. As soon as I hopped out, I always went to apologize to them for spoiling their peace. It's not so great walking for four hours to escape humanity, only to find a dirty great helicopter hovering ten feet above your flask before depositing someone who runs around like a maniac shouting into a walkie talkie. So I would nip over, tell them what we were up to and grovel a bit. Their response never varied. 'So that's how you do these shows, is it? Most of us have to walk up.'

Given the experiences of the shoot thus far, my first instinct was to resort to swift and immediate violence, but these were viewers and one is contractually bound to be reasonably pleasant. So I carried on throughout the

summer like an apprentice Anneka Rice, taking good-
natured abuse from every Munro-climber in Britain, with
my teeth gritted. I did at one point contemplate having
a card printed that I could simply hand to the doubting
Thomases on the slopes. It would read, 'Shut your face,
dog breath. I've climbed it twice already'. On reflection,
however, I decided it might not show advanced public
relations skills on my part and settled on smiling and
waving instead.

Helicopters are expensive things, and since our budget
was as tight as Billy Idol's pants, it was important to get
the most out of our time. This meant that after the shot
had been completed of me walking at a leisurely pace
along a mountain top, trying to remember what I did
three weeks ago when we filmed it from the ground,
I would have to sprint back to the chopper to get to
the next location without delay. Wasting time getting
in and out meant money lost. By the time we were at
location two, my heart was trying to knock a hole in
my vest and I was starting to hallucinate. The worst one
of all, of course, was a return to the In Pin. This meant
being dumped at the base and climbing the whole thing
again, but this time with a helicopter roaring only yards
away. The only delight was on my return to the car park.
The chopper dumped me, still wearing all the climbing
gear, and went back to pick up Ross. I spoke to the pilot
with a walkie talkie and reminded them to get a shot of
the path on the way back down. As I started to undo all
the strange and mysterious straps, a man approached me
in a very polite, reverential way. I'm not used to being
approached like this. Normally people either shout 'Hoi,

are you that thin bint on the telly?' or they simply point and laugh. This man clearly had some respect.

'Excuse me,' he said, practically bowing. Things were looking up in ego land. 'Is there an exercise on today, or is it a real emergency?'   .

I looked blankly at him, trying to decipher the sentence. With enormous disappointment, my brain collated the information and came back with the solution that this man thought I was a Mountain Rescue person. I caught sight of myself reflected in the car window, peroxide blonde hair, pink lipstick and legs like sticks, and couldn't help wondering what this man must imagine the rest of the Mountain Rescue team might look like.

'No. No emergency,' was all I could manage, but he had certainly made my day. I strutted around in the car park in a manly fashion for a few more minutes before taking off the climbing gear, just in case somebody else thought I was in the Mountain Rescue team. I was on the point of thinking of growing a beard when somebody pointed and laughed. It was business as usual and I hid in the car.

A VIDEO COMPILATION OF THE FIRST SERIES.

AVAILABLE FROM ALL MAJOR VIDEO RETAIL OUTLETS

A production adapted for video by